Showing Kunga

From Pet Owner to Dog Show Junkie

Alxe Noden

Wenatchee, WA

Showing Kunga
From Pet Owner to Dog Show Junkie
Alxe Noden

Dogwise Publishing
A Division of Direct Book Service, Inc.
403 South Mission Street, Wenatchee, Washington 98801
509-663-9115, 1-800-776-2665
www.dogwisepublishing.com / info@dogwisepublishing.com

Cover photo: Karen Evasuik
Interior photographs: Cindy Davis, Martin Mosko, Alxe Noden, Karen Evasuik

ISBN 978-1-61781-078-7

Library of Congress Cataloging-in-Publication Data
Noden, Alxe.
Showing Kunga : from pet owner to dog show junkie / Alxe Noden.
p. cm.
ISBN 978-1-61781-078-7
1. Dog shows--United States. 2. Great Dane--United States. 3. Noden, Alxe. 4. Dog owners--United States--Biography. I. Title.
SF425.N73 2012
791.8--dc23
2012002209

Printed in the U.S.A.

More praise for *Showing Kunga*

At last! A completely honest and exposed view into the exhilarating, crazy, and often baffling world of conformation dog showing. As a newcomer to the sport, Alxe learns (often the hard way) about the competitiveness, the etiquette, and the unwritten rules of the ring, and shares her experiences and faux pas so that her readers may have a "leg up" on their competition. With seemingly no subject off-limits, the reader follows Alxe on her journey from a novice pet owner to championed show handler. Conformation showing motivates us to train and gives us an activity to do with our dog. However in the end, a ribbon is worth 39-cents, but the shared experiences with our dogs are priceless.

Kyra Sundance, World-renowned trainer, bestselling author of 6 books including *101 Dog Tricks* and host of an award winning DVD series.

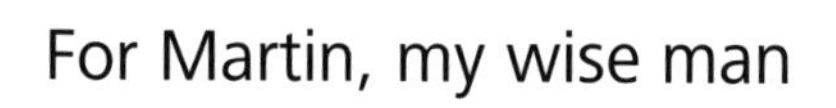
For Martin, my wise man

Table of Contents

ACKNOWLEDGMENTS

I have met so many helpful and interesting people during this journey that in trying to name them all I'll undoubtedly miss someone and regret it. So let me first thank everyone who has taught me something about dogs or helped me with Kunga, from giving me tips on handling, grooming, and care, to holding him ringside.

Cindy Davis of Della Danes was the first person to get me thinking about showing a dog, so I should put the blame for being bitten by the show bug squarely on her shoulders! Thanks to Cindy for letting me have Kunga and providing hours of breeder support and lots of good advice.

The Great Dane Club of Greater Denver is a splendid example of what a breed club can be. Its members have encouraged me and scolded me for my mistakes and made me a better handler in a shorter time than anyone could have thought possible considering the raw material. Kathryn Kudron was the first person other than Kunga's breeder to think he might be show quality, and I appreciate her continued advice and inspiration. Carol and Don Volleberg taught me most of what I know about showing, always making sure that I didn't get too upset at my mistakes or too full of myself when Kunga won. Don ably handled Kunga to about half his points, including his first major, which was a big factor in our success. Loren Bengston, Craig and Sally Lynn, Kelley Martin, Liam and Kristin O'Leary, Celeste Perkins, John Collums, Josh Saunders, Terri and Cindy Million, and all the other members of the club, have added to my enjoyment of this sport and knowledge about Danes. Without meeting these people first—and discovering their kindness and basic sanity despite their loony love for their dogs—I would never have considered trying to show Kunga.

Thanks to the people who agreed to be interviewed for this book and taught me something about dogs and showing them: Michael Brantley, Lisa Befus, Linda Cain, Mari Lynn Davisson, Virginia Perry Gardiner, Lisa Goodman, Barbara Gresser, Janie Healy, Lori Kamrath, Lindsey Kamrath, Brenda Lott, Elmer Robinson, Mary Rogers, Rita Suddharth, and Debbie Towndrow. There were many others I met at shows whose names I never knew who told me stories and taught me to look at dogs: thanks to all of you.

Thank you to David Frei and his able staff at the Westminster Kennel Club for helping me to make my way at the annual show in 2011 and for introducing me to some wonderful people.

Thank you to the Woodwards and to the fine people at Dogwise, who each in their own way made this a better book.

I can't thank my husband Martin Mosko enough for his comments on this book, his huge heart, and his wisdom. He never fails to surprise and delight with his humor, his insight, and his patience. This book would not have been possible without him.

CHAPTER 1

Got Dog?

Kunga at about six weeks old. Photo by Cindy Davis.

The room service waiter arrived quickly after my call, with a parfait glass of vanilla ice cream and a long-handled spoon on a tray. As I signed the chit, he wished me good evening and said he hoped I'd enjoy the dessert.

"Oh, it's not for me," I said. "It's for my dog."

Not until I saw his look of astonishment did I realize quite how ridiculous this sounded.

"Well, he won't eat his dinner, and he has a show tomorrow, and sometimes if you just mix in a little ice cream, he'll gobble the rest down with it," I tried to explain.

The waiter just took back the check and went off down the hall, taking his disbelief with him. I realized I'd just had another of those dog show moments, things that are perfectly ordinary in this strange world that seem ludicrous to outsiders. There have been a lot of these since I decided to show Kunga.

Kunga is my young Great Dane. When I brought him home he was 22 pounds and destined to be my pet dog. Eight months later he weighed more than 120 pounds and I was walking him into a show ring. This book is the story of how my pet became a show dog, and how I got hooked on this strange and sometimes wonderful world of showing. It will give you a sense of how to get into showing dogs, and what you can expect once you start.

There are some magical moments in showing, great wins that set your heart racing. There is also a lot of work and expense, and you'll make some dispiriting discoveries about the unfortunate lengths some people will go in order to beat the competition. I've met wonderful people and I've met some terrible people. Like almost anyone who shows a dog, I found mentors who helped and encouraged me, and sadly

I've met people who have dismayed me with their backbiting and small-mindedness. I've spent a surprising amount of money on things I'd never imagined, and I've had the rewarding experience of spending a lot of time with my dog. The ups and downs of showing are not for everyone, but I enjoy it enough that I'm still trotting my big blue boy into the show ring.

I didn't grow up around dog shows. Though my family had many dogs while I was growing up, they were mostly mutts until my mother began her infatuation with Great Danes. We had a succession of rescued Danes in our house after that, and I fell in love with these gorgeous goofball dogs. My family's Danes were fawns and brindles. The fawns are a tawny gold color, generally with black markings on the nose (called a "mask") and around the ears; the brindles are a darker gold with an overlay of black striations through their coats. These are probably the most popular two colors for Danes, but there are others as well. My husband and I once had a harlequin, which is a white dog with ragged black and grey patches all over. The American Kennel Club also recognizes black, blue, and mantle colors for the show ring, mantle being a black dog with a white collar and additional white, usually on its head, chest and feet. Sometimes you see a color called merle, which is a grayish variation on harlequin, but this color (together with other colors like "fawnikin") is not acceptable in the show ring.

After our harlequin Dane died, it was a few years before I looked for another dog. At first I didn't have a specific color of Dane in mind; I pretty much like them all. That is, until I saw my first Blue. Blue Danes are relatively rare out here in the Rocky Mountain region, and aren't really very popular among breeders elsewhere, either. But when I had my first sight of one, I was smitten by that steel blue coat color.

I didn't get Kunga to be a show dog. When I began searching for dogs, I was only looking for a family pet to join our young Bloodhound, Lucy. In fact, until I went to my first show myself, I had never even seen a real dog show. I'd watched the Group and Best in Show judging from Westminster on TV once or twice, but had no idea how the dogs got there or what the basis was for judging them. Like many, I'd seen the mockumentary "Best in Show," and that movie formed the only information I had about the people and the process of showing. If anything, I thought those who showed dogs must be crazy, neurotic, mean-spirited people with more money than sense. I had the vague sense that show dogs were highly trained but not deeply loved, and that they lived comfortably but not normally. When I first got Kunga, I had absolutely no intention or interest in getting involved in showing.

I didn't intend to get a show dog, but I did decide to go to a reputable breeder rather than wait for a rescue dog or get a puppy from a backyard breeder. Danes grow eccentrically large, astonishingly fast, which can produce a really distressing range of health problems. If you don't start with a structurally correct dog that is likely to be free of genetic defects (all reputable breeders do health checks before breeding), you often wind up with an unhealthy dog that may end up costing you much more than the purchase price.

When I started looking, I found that there were plenty of pretty dog pictures on breeder web sites. It's not easy to know where to place your trust, though, since anyone can design a web site with nice photos and claim to have great dogs. How can you know which breeders will have healthy and temperamentally sound puppies and which are essentially puppy mills? There was not much information on this issue that I could find. The laws that license breeders are pretty sketchy, and I couldn't locate a central database that lists breeders who have been fined or otherwise penalized for violating laws on dog cruelty. I didn't know any breeders I could turn to for advice, either. (See the Appendix for how I'd go about looking for a puppy based on what I know today.)

Since I didn't have a clue what to look for or how to find a reputable breeder, I began sorting out breeders and web sites according to who showed their dogs and had produced winners. Even though I didn't want a show dog, I figured the people with award-winning dogs would be invested in having healthy puppies and maintaining their reputation even with their non-showing, or "pet quality" dogs. In every litter, even those from great champions, there are inevitably going to be great dogs and lesser dogs. The great ones the breeders sell to people who will show them, and the lesser ones get sold to people like me who just want a pet around the house.

To my good fortune, I ran across the web site of Della Danes in Cape Coral, Florida. The owner, Cindy Davis, I came to know as a relentlessly positive person bouncing with energy. This is a woman who once bred her dog even though she knew the puppies would arrive right at the time she would be giving birth to her first child. Nothing seems to faze Cindy. She just pulls her long blonde hair into a ponytail and sails in to solve any problem that presents itself. She had started breeding fawn Danes and later moved into blues. Some of the puppies she had bred were being shown successfully. And when I was searching for a dog, she happened to have a blue female, the daughter of one of the winningest blue show dogs ever in the U.S., who was pregnant with puppies.

Cindy was no pushover. Like any good breeder, she was pleased to hear how much I liked the pictures of her lovely girl Storm, the prospective mama, but she had the proper degree of skeptical interest in my background. Had I owned a Great Dane before? Would I have enough room in my house and yard for a big dog? Was I home a lot or gone for many hours a day? Did I have any idea how expensive it is to raise a Dane? I had to fill out a long questionnaire just to get to talk to Cindy about acquiring one of her puppies.

Cindy had bred her girl (females are known universally in the dog world as "bitches"—please don't be offended as I use this term throughout this book) to a male from Australia who was from the famous Thunderfire line of blue Danes. The puppies would owe a lot to Federal Express for getting frozen semen from halfway across the world. The sire, Australian Champion Thunderfire's Law N' Order, is a handsome fellow with a huge head and a great big chest.

I'd made it clear to Cindy right from the start that I didn't intend to show my dog. I knew that showing was expensive and time-consuming, and I already had a life. I very much wanted another dog, though, and once the level of my commitment and experience with Danes was established to her satisfaction, Cindy agreed to sell me a puppy—*if* there were enough boys in the litter, that is. There was another person ahead of me in line for a male puppy from this breeding. Since you never know how many puppies there will be, and of which sex, all I could do was anticipate the whelping day.

Waiting was awful, but finally, late in the evening of April 2, 2008, my little blue boy arrived in the world along with seven other puppies, a total of five girls and three boys. Each received a colored string tied loosely around their necks to identify them. Puppies look a lot alike, especially when very small, so these colored strings—replaced as they grow bigger by the same colored collar—help to keep them all straight.

All puppies are astonishingly cute, but I fell in love with the male wearing the black collar immediately. Cindy had specifically warned all her prospective owners not to do this, since we wouldn't know who got which pup until they were nearly ready to leave. This had surprised me when I first heard about the practice, but the breeders know what they're doing. The pups are like little russet potatoes when they're born, sort of shapeless and helpless, with nubby ears and pink paw pads. The breeder needs time to assess each puppy's personality and potential for the show ring, so that those destined for a show home are of a better quality. This is an almost mystical process and not at all an exact science, though there are many puppy evaluation methods for structure, temperament, and movement that work with varying success. Stories abound of breeders who keep the "pick of the litter" for themselves, only to wind up with a nice but not extraordinary dog, while an overlooked littermate goes on to show ring glory with someone else.

I didn't know how to assess a dog for the show ring, and I didn't care. "Black collar boy" was a roly-poly puppy who just seemed to call to me from the web page photos. He was smiling in his three-week-old pictures even though his eyes weren't open yet. As soon as we were allowed to express a preference, I put my dibs on him.

Two of the three boys in the litter were deemed to be of show quality; one was wearing a blue collar, and the other was the boy I had fallen for wearing the black collar. Cindy wanted to be sure that the first person in line, who wanted a show dog, received the puppy best suited to the ring. Cindy consulted with many other breeders and constantly observed the developing pups' structures and personalities in order to make a recommendation. I know she even sent photos to Australia for the owner of the sire to look at. I was thrilled when they all agreed: the blue collar boy was the best prospect for show. The woman with first choice took him, and the little black collar boy was mine.

The litter had a "law" theme. Cindy asked that all the puppies have an AKC registered name that had something to do with law, in homage to the sire. Since he came from Della Danes, my black collar boy became Della's Pro Bono. (Other owners had a blast with this law theme: littermates include "Della's Beyond a Reasonable Doubt" and "Della's Above the Law.") His call name—what we say when we talk to him—is Kunga, which means "joyful one" in Tibetan.

At the standard age of eight weeks old (when pups have passed certain crucial socialization milestones within their dog families), Cindy loaded Kunga into a crate, drove an hour or so to the airport, and consigned him to the tender care of the airline. He had to wait in an air-conditioned van before being loaded into the baggage compartment and flown to Houston. There, crate and dog changed planes to connect to Denver. When I finally finished signing paperwork and was able to let the poor pup out of the crate on some lawn near the cargo building, I thought he'd be a wreck. Instead, Kunga bounded out of the crate, looked around curiously, and peed on the spot. He looked up at me with his bright blue eyes, as if to ask, "OK, what's next?" On the 45-minute drive home he sniffed at my husband as he drove, then settled down peaceably and fell asleep in my lap. I was already in love with him.

Kunga when I first got him.

Though Kunga's steel-blue color was lovely from the beginning, his development was herky-jerky and he sure didn't look like a show quality dog. Some weeks, his hind end was taller than the front, and other weeks it was the other way around. His head was so big it looked like it was made for another body. I was a bit mystified when Cindy insisted he was going to be a good-looking boy. My husband and I kept shaking our heads over this as he grew—fast—into a leggy five-month-old. His personality began to show itself, too. He was game for anything, and curious, nosing into people, woodpiles, partly closed doors, and kitchen cabinets. The only things I ever saw disturb him were the vacuum cleaner and the lawn mower, but even with those mechanical monsters, he barked furiously and tried to drive them away rather than running in the opposite direction.

As Kunga approached the age when I'd usually neuter a male pup, Cindy asked if I'd be willing to let him keep his testicles (the polite phrase is to "keep him intact") until he was old enough to have his semen collected and frozen for later breedings. Though I didn't intend to show him, Cindy wanted to be sure that his DNA continued on, and she wanted to use it in her breeding program. I wasn't at all sure I wanted to hold off on neutering, especially when I'd heard just how difficult having an intact male could be. I was hesitant from the start to have to limit Kunga to a life walked on-leash only in certain areas, which is pretty much what he would be constrained to as an intact, dominant male. But Cindy believed strongly that my funny-looking boy was going to be very nicely shaped, and she was willing to part with the cash to get a piece of his future by having a vet collect his semen.

Could it really be that I had a dog of show quality? I wanted to be sure that Kunga was going to be a good enough dog to be worth breeding if I was going to keep him intact and deal with the limitations that implied. I wanted a second opinion about this from someone who knew what they were talking about, but who didn't have any stake in him. I didn't want to have a rambunctious hormonal male without a pretty good reason. I still didn't intend to show Kunga, but I was willing to keep him intact for a while if he looked like it would be a good idea to keep his genes in the pool.

I didn't have any idea who to ask about this. If you've just had pet dogs, it never occurs to you to wonder what it might take for your dog to win in a show ring. Of course your own dog is the most beautiful one on earth—to you. Of course he is the best possible animal ever made—in your opinion. But I had no idea how to decide whether Kunga or his progeny actually had a chance in the show ring.

To do research on show ring requirements, you can start by reading the "standard" for the breed. This is the official measure of what's considered desirable for your breed, written by the national breed club and adopted by the American Kennel Club. The standard is a detailed description of all the important parts of the dog and what the AKC believes each part should look like. It also describes how the dog should move and its preferred temperament. Even our pampered puppies were originally bred for a purpose, and the standard demands that the couch-potato dogs still conform to the underlying purpose of their breed. You can find copies of the written standard by going to the web site for your national breed club (for Danes that's the Great Dane Club of America: http://www.gdca.org, go to "About" and then "official standard"), or on the AKC web site (http://www.akc.org, go to "breed information" and then under "about AKC breeds," choose the breed you're interested in).

Though the standards are written in more or less plain English (you may have to look up a few anatomical terms), it's still pretty difficult to decide whether your particular dog comes close to the standard unless you've seen a lot of dogs in your breed. If you suddenly decide your pet dog would be a world-beater in the show ring, you should do as I did: get an opinion from someone experienced at evaluating dogs who will tell you honestly whether your dog is show-ring quality. You probably shouldn't take the word of your obedience trainer or your best friend or your mother, unless one of those people has had many years in the breed. If your dog has come from a "backyard breeder"—someone who does no health checks, does not show their dogs, and just breeds for the cash they can get—it's not terribly likely that you have a quality dog that's going to do much winning in the beauty contest of conformation. If you acquired your dog from the pound or from a rescue, he almost certainly does not have his AKC registration (required to enter the dog in shows), and probably has been spayed or neutered, which precludes you from showing in conformation. Hey, no problem: you can still train your dog as a therapy dog or to do tricks that impress your friends. You just can't take him into the conformation show ring at a sanctioned kennel club event.

But if you got your dog from a reputable breeder, he has full AKC registration, and you think he could be show quality, look for someone else who can tell you whether or not that's true. Where to find those people? You could start by finding breeders near you and asking to visit their home or kennel to learn more about their breed. Most will be happy to have you come and see their dogs and tell you their views on the breed; some might even be willing to evaluate your pup for you. Keep in mind, however, that every breeder has her own preferences and prejudices.

You could also go to a dog show near you and find the ring where your breed is showing. Almost anyone holding a dog will be happy to talk your ear off about the breed and tell you where to find more information. But you can't bring a dog to a show that isn't entered in the classes, so don't bring your puppy to the show in the hopes he'll be evaluated right there and then.

Since I had no idea how to find a dog show near me, I hunted around on-line until I found the Great Dane Club of Greater Denver, which is what's known as a "breed club." Almost every region and big city has a club of people interested in any given breed. The members are almost all breeders themselves, or have show dogs they hope to breed one day. Often the club's main purpose is to put together a specialty show—a beauty contest for their own breed only—but they also debate how best to improve the breed and educate the public about it. These clubs are filled with people who show their dogs and breed their dogs and know a lot about their breed. And they are all very opinionated! As my husband points out, it's also one of the few places you can go to a meeting and tell endless stories about your dogs and have other people listen.

I'd laughed at the movies I'd seen about showing. I'd read a couple of how-to-show books, and heard the warnings about the backbiting, gossip, politics, and general nastiness of show people. I wasn't sure anyone would even talk to me, much less give me an honest opinion on my dog's quality. I was nervous when I tracked down the club secretary and asked to attend a meeting.

At the next monthly gathering, I walked in with gangly five-month old Kunga to general cries of delight. These are dog people, after all, and they adore puppies. Nearly everyone had dog treats tucked into their pockets or purses. All of them had to have some loving-up time and their share of dog slobber, which Kunga produces in large amounts when he's excited. I thought all this petting and playing was sweet. I learned later that it's also part of the evaluation process.

As they played with Kunga and offered him treats, the members of the club were assessing his temperament. Danes should not be withdrawn or frightened, nor should they be openly aggressive without provocation. Was Kunga nervous with all the attention of a whole room of people, did he dislike being touched, was he likely to nip? Each of these would be a drawback in the show ring. Happily, Kunga is an outgoing and curious fellow, and he enjoyed the whole event immensely. His tail was up and wagging and he gave almost everyone the gentle *huff* of air that constitutes his greeting. There was the added bonus that he didn't pee on the meeting room floor.

At the end of the meeting, one member stayed to talk with me for a few minutes. Kathryn has had several breeds of dogs in her time, including Danes, and had evaluated a lot of puppies. She agreed to go over Kunga with me to see how closely he fit the standard. Kathryn, like all experienced people in the show ring, has definite opinions. And she is straightforward and plainspoken, especially about dogs. I got an earful about Kunga's faults at the time. His back was still "roached" (he had an upward curve in it until he was about 8 months old). His shoulders were a bit too straight. His tail curled up into the air rather than being held low and slightly curved, like a scimitar. But, Kathryn pointed out, he had excellent angles at his back end, wonderful tight feet (the standard calls for "catlike" feet), a marvelous big head, and a great disposition. She also cautioned me that five and a half months is a terrible time to evaluate dogs, as they often appear awkward and ungainly at that age.

Some things about him, like his back, could grow better or he could get worse, though basic structure doesn't change. I hadn't realized until Kathryn told me so that having a blue dog might be a problem in the show ring: they're not that popular with judges. More problematic was the issue of Kunga's ears, which are "natural," meaning they were left the way he had them when he was born. Many Dane show dogs are "cropped," a surgical procedure in which about a third of the ear is cut off, and the remainder cut into a triangular shape with a point at the end. Afterward, the ears are taped up and wrapped around posts or a plastic cup for anywhere from a few months to a year. This gives the electrified ears-up look that many judges have grown up with and continue to prefer. (This surgery is prohibited in many countries of Europe, Australia, New Zealand, and South Africa, among other nations, and you cannot show your dog in these countries if the ears are cropped.) Overall, though, Kathryn's general opinion was that Kunga was pretty certainly "show quality," good-looking enough to be more than a pet.

Kathryn with her Saint Bernard, "Trekkie," UR02 Sleepyhollow's Starstruck Voyage, RN CD CGC.

I mulled all this over with my husband. After a lot of consideration, we decided we would keep Kunga intact until he could give a semen sample for artificial insemination, which would probably be at about a year old. This was due in large part to the fact that my breeder Cindy had been very helpful and kind, and she really wanted to see Kunga's genes continue. She was responsible, she was not breeding just to make money, and she genuinely thought Kunga was a quality dog. Though Kathryn had pointed out some of his faults, she too thought Kunga was going to be a pretty handsome guy.

Once we made the decision that we'd keep Kunga intact for at least a few more months, I decided to explore this world of dog showing. Before I went to the club meeting, I hadn't even considered it. But once I met Kathryn and the others, I discovered they were fanatics about Danes but not loony in general. In fact, I was intrigued and impressed by the people

I'd met there, who were welcoming and kind, not at all what I'd expected. I also enjoy competition: I showed horses in riding and jumping competitions when I was a teen, and I fenced for my university fencing team in college and tournament competition. Once I thought my dog would have a serious chance, and I found I liked the people I met in the sport, my interest spiked in getting Kunga out there to compete with other dogs.

I hadn't planned on showing Kunga and didn't know whether I could do it myself. I didn't know what kind of preparation I'd need, but I'd found a lot of help through the Dane breed club, and Kunga seemed to like the attention. It would be a great way to spend time with my dog. So though it was far from my original intention, I sort of stumbled into showing.

At first it wasn't serious: I thought I might learn something, meet some new friends and have a good time. Nothing big, I thought, just some local shows that would give us both a quick taste of competition and something fun to do on weekends for a few months. Then I could get Kunga's semen collected and he could go back to being "just a dog."

Wrong.

CHAPTER 2
Starting Out

There are a lot of us who get into showing without planning to, like the woman I met in the stands at a show in Topeka, Kansas. Her husband had always wanted a German Shepherd, and she finally bought him a nice bitch as a present. He was so proud of her and so convinced she was show quality that they decided to take her to handling classes so they could learn to show her and win lots of ribbons. There, they learned the bitch had some major faults with her conformation, but they had so much fun learning about handling and the breed that they kept going despite losing. They had good mentors who helped them find another dog—this one of good quality—and they showed that one to a championship, then decided to do it again. And again…now they are successful German Shepherd breeders and have their own RV to travel to shows everywhere in the country. They've even seen one of the dogs they bred take a coveted Best in Show award. But, as the woman told me, they didn't intend to have a life dominated by dog shows. They just sort of fell into it, "like everybody does," she said.

That was my experience: I didn't buy Kunga to show him, but circumstances conspired to get us both into the show ring.

Conformation shows were originally dog beauty contests, put on by fanciers as lighthearted competitions for bragging rights. The first dog show in England appears to have been held in 1859, an outgrowth of the gentry's desire to compete for owner of the best purebred dog. Not until 1873 did the English form The Kennel Club, which tried to impose some order on these social events by coming up with rules and breed standards. The Kennel Club also began publishing a Stud Book, with lists of winning dogs. This was the real reason for all the regulations and classifications: to establish which dogs and bitches would be best for breeding. It's still the primary stated reason for showing dogs, which is why show dogs can't be neutered or spayed until after they're done showing.

The American Kennel Club was formed in 1884 and began certifying dog shows, accrediting judges, and registering dogs as belonging to a specific breed. The AKC sanctions several kinds of shows, including obedience (showing how well the dog follows commands), agility (running dogs through courses to test their speed, balance, and courage), and conformation. The latter are the contests in which dogs are appraised by judges familiar with the breed to see how closely they conform to an ideal breed standard.

Unlike many people with their first dog, I didn't think Kunga could be a superstar. I just wanted to have fun showing him while I was waiting for him to become mature enough to collect semen and be neutered. But I'd never been to a dog show and didn't understand how to get started. My friend Kathryn, who had assessed Kunga at the club meeting, suggested I enroll in a handling class to learn about showing.

Handling classes are the perfect way to introduce yourself and your puppy to the dog show world. There are many rules and regulations about showing—some of them unwritten! —and a great deal of skill that goes into the actual handling in the ring. You can always tell a newbie at a show: they're the ones who lead a dog into the ring with a metal choke chain or a fabric collar with a thick lead from a pet store, who don't know how to set up their dog for examination, or how to move around the ring. Any of these things mark you as a rank amateur with a pet rather than a show dog, and it will be difficult to overcome this first impression even with a fantastic dog at the other end of the lead. To make sure your dog doesn't end up looking green your first few times in the ring, seek out a handling class in your area (your breed club people will know who teaches them, or you can Google them) and attend at least of few of them to learn the basics. That's how I found my friend Carol at Rocwind Canine Center.

Carol has been breeding, training, and showing Great Danes for decades, even showing one of her own to Best of Winners at the Westminster Dog show. She isn't much taller than I am—maybe about 5'3"—but she is much stronger. Her work-toughened hands tell the story of her time spent with dogs and horses. Carol is direct and decisive. She'll think of something nice to say even if she doesn't think much of your dog, but she'll never lie if you ask her point-blank if the dog is show quality or not. Though she can be gentle with frightened or abused dogs, she doesn't put up with nonsense from her animals or the people who handle them. She has been a great mentor for me in the Dane breed.

If you watch dog shows on TV but haven't shown yourself, you might think the handler's job is pretty easy. After all, it appears to the layperson that they just walk the dog up to the judge, stand them up in a show stance—called a "stack"—and wait for the judge to examine the dog before running them up and down the side of the ring and then around to the end of the line. Simple, right?

You learn differently when you try this yourself. First of all, no one has explained to the puppy what you have in mind. When we began, Kunga had no particular interest in standing still in any kind of stance, much less the stack. The first time we went to handling class we created a circus all by ourselves. He was about seven months old and 100 pounds, large enough to be difficult to persuade to do anything he didn't want to do. With all the dogs around—none neutered or spayed—he mostly wanted to meet the other canines and avoid the instructor's hands as we practiced the "examination." This is when the judge (or in the handling class, the instructor) puts her hands on all parts of the dog, examines his teeth, and feels his condition and bone structure. Kunga danced sideways, he leaned on me, he backed up away from the collar, he turned in circles, he pulled his head sideways, and generally led me a jolly dance. I was embarrassed to have the worst behaved puppy in the class, although we certainly provided a lot of comic relief for the other students.

As part of the examination, the judge is required to touch the dog's scrotum to be certain there are two testicles, both properly in position. It's not easy to convince a dog to stand quietly while a total stranger gets intimate with him, and there isn't a boy alive that takes to having his testicles stroked by a stranger without some objection. But the dog must learn to be still and take all this with composure. In fact, the Great Dane standard calls for a bold but friendly demeanor, so a dog that shies from having his head touched, or is grouchy about having his rear examined, is not demonstrating the correct temperament. Really bad behavior, like growling at the judge or turning to bite as the rear is examined, will get the dog dismissed from the class. Puppies get a bit of leeway for friskiness, but aggression is never tolerated.

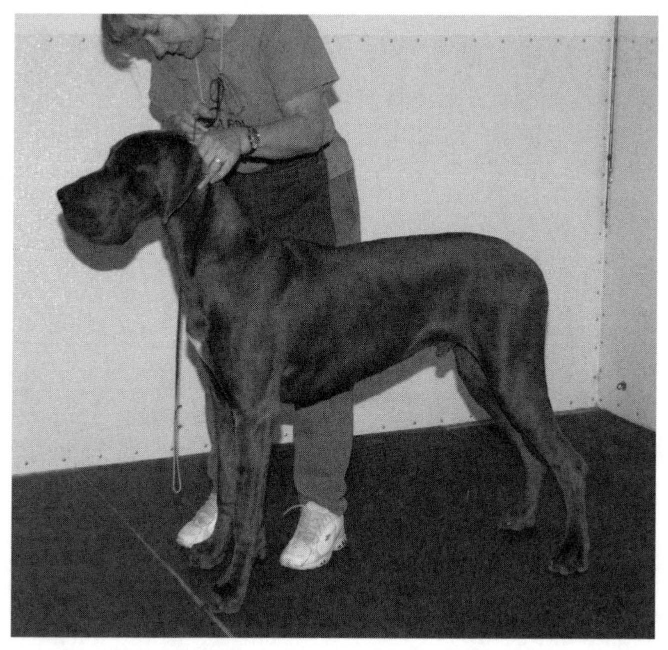

My friend Carol teaching Kunga the show stack. At the time, Kunga was eight months old.

Kunga learned the stack pretty quickly. Looking at his teeth also didn't take too long to teach. The rear examination, however, was our downfall. Kunga would back up, sit, or turn around indignantly at the first touch at the back of his legs. This isn't too unusual, but I was puzzled by the challenge of getting him to accept the examination without fussing. One early trick I learned was to put my outstretched arm under him, about two-thirds of the way back on his tummy, which kept him from sitting down or moving forward. But this was not a long-term winning strategy with a Dane that soon would weigh half again as much as I did: he'd just slump down and push me down with him. Carol recommended what she called the "pecker pinch," which is pretty much what it sounds like: when the dog is standing up, you quickly and lightly pinch his sheath. It causes most dogs to throw out their chest and stand straighter on their legs in sheer surprise. Unfortunately, it didn't work with Kunga. He was just more insulted.

The only solution to his indignation seemed to be time and repetition. I got some very strange looks as I tried to recruit friends to help with this particular training. Generally, people are willing to help with training a dog to sit nicely at the door or lie down when there's company. But they give you funny looks when you ask them if they could please lightly stroke your dog's testicles. It was my first taste of disconnect, the first time that what in the show world is "ordinary" clashed with real-world behavior.

In addition to the physical examination, the judge also wants to see your dog move. Every breed has a different way of moving, evolved from the original use of the dog. Danes, which were bred as estate guard dogs and boar hunters, should move smoothly, with no rolling of the top-line, and display a long, reaching gait with no "flipping" out of the paws. A Bulldog has a completely different gait, described in its standard as "peculiar, his gait being a loose-jointed, shuffling, sidewise motion, giving the characteristic 'roll.'" The handler's job is to make sure the speed and direction of the movement are controlled to show off the dog's gait in the best light, no matter what the breed.

Every judge has her own way of moving the dogs in the ring. Though the patterns include the "triangle" and the even less common "L," (trust me, you don't want to have to do the latter), the most common pattern is "down and back" on the diagonal. Starting from the judge, you trot your dog toward the corner of the ring, turn around, and trot back. How hard can this be?

Somehow Kunga and I managed to murder the down-and-back. At first he wanted to run faster than I could, dragging me along behind like a kite. When I finally convinced him he had to wait for me, he bobbed and weaved back and forth. If I let the lead get too long, he would begin to pull away from me; if I yanked on him to get him back, he'd lean toward me, right into the path I was taking. The first time he did this, I took an entirely predictable header over the top of him, causing the whole handling class to "Oooooh" in horrified delight as I hit the ground. I think everyone was just glad there was one dork in the class less coordinated than they were! This is one of the reasons you should take a handling class, so that these foolish mistakes get made during practice rather than when a real judge is rolling her eyes, eager to get you out of her ring.

At the very beginning of each down and back (or whatever pattern the judge assigns), most handlers make what's called a "courtesy turn." They move from the judge's left side across the front of the judge to her right side, then make a turn clockwise to aim properly toward the other side of the ring. This is not too difficult with a smaller dog, but with a giant Dane in a small space it can be a challenge. Kunga nearly always spotted something behind the judge that he thought needed closer inspection. He would stop dead halfway through the turn, which I'd only realize after my arm jerked me to a stop as though I were a ship at anchor. This also provided some amusement to the other people in the handling class, since it usually had the effect of me reeling backward with a startled look on my face. I had to learn to anticipate this little maneuver with a light tap on Kunga's butt about halfway around the turn.

Another handling requirement that is far trickier than it looks is trying to get your dog to look at you and the judge with a bright, alert look. Usually this is accomplished by waving little treats (called "bait") in front of the dog at strategic moments. One sniff of liver or cheese or hot dog is often enough to get your dog's undivided attention. It does not guarantee, however, his complete cooperation. Most dogs will lean eagerly toward the treat with their ears down submissively, which is not at all what you want. Instead you want to present the bait as an inducement to stand still and focus on it.

Like everything, this takes training. With Kunga there was the additional difficulty that he didn't much care about even the tastiest treat when he was excited or distracted. I could bring primo steak bits into handling class and he would still turn them down in favor of looking around or dancing in a circle when he was supposed to be still. I resorted to using alternative bait: a squeaky toy. This worked sporadically, especially if deployed only once at a crucial time, like at the end of the down-and-back when the dog has to stand and offer that intense, regal Great Dane stare. Usually, Kunga stopped and gave his goofy, one ear back and one ear forward look, which is just not going to impress any judge. The squeaky toy would sometimes get those ears forward.

Teaching Kunga to pay attention with a piece of bait.

Kunga eventually settled down enough around all the other dogs in class that he learned to take bait treats. This made it easier to get a good, attentive look from him, but I learned the hard way that timing is crucial. He quickly figured out that I kept the treats in my right-hand pocket, and as soon as I reached for one on the move, he would unerringly swivel his head toward that pocket, right across my chest. This had the obvious disadvantage of bringing me to a full stop on the down and back, since a giant dog in search of treats can be surprisingly insistent that we concentrate on FOOD RIGHT NOW rather than this silly running back and forth. Carol clued me in that I should take the treat out of my pocket as we completed the courtesy turn and Kunga wasn't looking, but I couldn't hold it in my hand because he'd smell it.

"Put it in your mouth," Carol instructed, "then take it out just at the last moment at the end of the down-and-back."

Ewww. I don't like liver, hot dogs, or cheap cheese, and the stuff that's sold as bait is pretty disgusting stuff. My admiration for professional handlers who do this all day soared. Who knew you'd have to eat liver to make a living? I couldn't get used to doing this and didn't present a pretty sight as I trotted along gagging on some awful bit of bait. It had the added complication that if I was choking back bile, Kunga got worried and would turn and look at me to see what was wrong. The mouth trick just never worked for us, so I still carry the bait in my right pocket and have gotten pretty speedy at pulling it out just at the end. (Nearly every handler's pockets are stuffed with bait. You can always tell a show dog because when they first meet you they sniff your pockets rather than your crotch.)

An important part of the handling class was training me not to do stupid things to make Kunga look bad. I had to learn to take longer strides when running beside him around the ring so he could stretch out and not mince along. I had to learn to handle the bait so that I wouldn't distract him from what we were supposed to be doing. I was scolded when I took the middle of the mat as we ran down and back from the judge. Carol had to remind me that the dog was showing, not me, and he should have the best footing possible and the most attention. So much to keep in mind at one time!

Apart from learning how to stack and move the dog, you learn all the little important but unwritten rules of ring etiquette in handling class. You find out that if you wear flip-flops you're going to trip. You discover that a metal choke chain from the pet store is not correct ring attire for your dog, but that instead you'll need a show collar and leash appropriate to your breed, which you can generally only buy on-line or at the shows. (Hey, it's fun to shop!) You learn to turn to the person behind you if you're at the head of the line, and ask if they're ready before moving off to circle the ring when the judge asks you to move around together.

After a couple of months of handling class, I began to feel less like a complete idiot, and Kunga had sort of learned what the ring was all about. It was time for his first actual show.

CHAPTER 3
First Show

When Kunga finally seemed capable of getting through a class without making too much of a fool of himself or me, I started to look for a show to enter. There are a few ways to find a dog show, but none are easy if you're not in the dog world. I tried Googling "Colorado dog show" and came up with over 1.4 million hits. Infodog.com gave a good list of the state's shows, and I began clicking through them, trying to decipher the strange symbols and letters. I finally learned that "AB" stood for all-breed show, what we call a typical dog show, with conformation classes for all breeds. There is "O," which means obedience classes, "R" for rally, and "M" means that matches will also be offered. Matches are sanctioned events run by AKC rules, but the winners don't earn any points toward their championships. These are often events for puppies and new owner/handlers, competitions that allow the dogs and handlers to get used to the show ring without the pressure of points.

Each show is run by a superintendent, generally a private company, which is responsible for making sure all the rules are followed, settles conflicts, metes out punishments, and reports the official results. The trick is to find these companies. The AKC has a list of licensed superintendents on their web site at http://www.akc.org/events/conformation/superintendents.cfm. Hunt down the one that organizes shows in your area and download (or have them mail to you) a "Premium List" for the show you want to enter. This is an AKC required document filled with lots of tiny print that lists everything you need to know about the upcoming show: where it is; who the judges are for each breed; what rules will apply on the show grounds; where you can park; and where you can set up a grooming spot. If it's possible to reserve your grooming spot, there will be an application form to send in with payment—often with a different deadline than the entry for the show! There may also be a separate form for reserved parking. At the very end of the Premium List is the official entry form, which you have to fill out and either mail or fax into the superintendent's office by a deadline listed. Often you can enter on-line at the superintendent's web site as well. Entries close two and a half weeks before the show, so you can't just arrive the day of the show and expect to get entered.

For our first show, I entered Kunga for one day of a five-day cluster of shows held in Denver, Colorado. I figured one day was as much as either of us could handle for the first time. The day before the show, the buildings were opened midday to allow exhibitors to unload and set up their crates, exercise pens (called "ex-pens" and intended as places for the dogs to poop and pee), and grooming areas. My friends Carol and Don were nice enough to let me put a crate for Kunga in their area so I wouldn't feel quite so lost.

I drove to the show grounds on a cold February afternoon the day before Kunga was entered, with my husband along to help carry the crate, various crate supplies, and a grooming bag that would stay in the grooming area. We also brought Kunga so he could sniff around the place and get used to the idea of an enclosed space with lots of dogs in it, thinking that would make it easier for him the next day. The show building was huge and confusing, with multiple entries and winding corridors that led to unexpected things like empty horse stalls. Finally we found the unloading area for "open grooming"—the space set aside for getting your dog ready for the ring—where the grooming spaces, marked out with chalk on the cement floor, were first come, first served. We walked through auditorium-type doors into a vast, echoing room filled with barking dogs and talking people, the clanging of metal crates being erected, and huge table-top blowdriers aimed at wet dogs on grooming tables. This is the song of the dog show, an incessant upheaval of sound that would drive any peaceable person insane. I've come to love it, but at first it was overwhelming. Kunga, however, was not intimidated—his head was up, his ears forward, his brow was wrinkled with dog concentration. It took my husband's greater strength to keep him in line as we walked through the grooming area.

After a lengthy hunt, we found Carol and Don's set-up, complete with stacked crates, two grooming tables, grooming suitcase, and a table for a coffee maker and snacks. One chair was all that could fit into the area without encroaching on the aisle or nearby spaces. We found the empty spot they'd saved for Kunga, set up his crate, and went for a walk around.

Kunga is a very curious dog, interested in everything. He was energized as he danced along next to us through the open grooming to the "reserved" grooming (where the spaces are closer to the rings and you can buy an assigned space for the length of the show), and then finally to the show floor. Here the rings are set up back to back, with folding white knee-high baby gates separating one from another. Mats of rough green plastic covered the interior surface of each ring, offering a less slippery surface than the cement floors. Beside the entry gate for each ring was a table with chairs for the stewards, and a tall pole with a sign announcing the number of the ring. For some reason, the tables always seem to be blue-topped, and the ring numbers are black on yellow. Kunga sniffed the floors, the walls, the tables, the chairs, the baby gates—anything I'd let him at, he investigated assiduously. I didn't know whether he'd like the floor covering, so we trotted into one of the empty rings and went around once. Then I show stacked him so he'd get the feeling of doing it in the ring. Satisfied, I walked him out of the ring, only to meet a large, stern fellow who didn't look pleased.

"Don't let the show officials see you doing that," he said.

"Doing what?" I asked.

"No one is allowed in the rings except during the classes," he said stiffly, then moved off.

I thought this was pretty ridiculous, since it was the day before anything would start and it couldn't possibly hurt to walk Kunga around inside the ring. However, I found it in the Premium List of rules later: "Dogs allowed in rings during judging only." Wow, there I was jeopardizing Kunga's show career and it hadn't even begun!

The show world is filled with these unexpected rules. There are some that make sense, like the one that the official show veterinarian can excuse any dog that she feels endangers the health of other dogs. If you show up with a dog that has kennel cough, for example, you're putting all the other dogs at risk, and the show should be able to stop you. There are other rules, like not letting your dog in the ring the day before the show when no one is using it, that to me seem kind of crazy.

There are plenty of rules about showing that are ignored or fudged, and others that are truly strict with violations earning you a suspension or even expulsion from the show. The trick is to learn which rules are real and which are mostly not enforced.

The grooming rules are among those where boundaries get pushed. Technically, a handler may not do anything artificial to the dog to improve his or her appearance. However, the Poodle people all use hair spray and mousse to make those mounds of hair stand up nicely, and I think nearly every dog that has white on its coat has had chalk rubbed through the hair and combed out to make the color bright and to color any darker skin beneath the hair. One handler friend of mine tells his students that you don't have to chalk your dog, "but the dog you lose to has usually been chalked." Danes often go gray around the muzzle prematurely, especially the fawns with black markings on their noses and eyes. Though in the standard, gray is perfectly acceptable and judges are instructed to disregard it, many feel that it puts the gray-haired dog at a disadvantage. Some people dye the mask hair to avoid the problem. Done well (and it's done in many other breeds, too), it is unnoticeable. But I've heard of it done so poorly that the judge comes away from the teeth exam with black covering his hands. This will get you sent out of the ring by an unhappy judge. Mascara is used to nice effect on certain longer-haired breeds of dogs: I saw this in grooming areas everywhere from little fairground shows in Colorado all the way to the national-level Westminster show.

Other, more serious alterations will get the handler suspended, especially if they involve surgery to fix perceived structural problems. Yet these rules are often ignored, especially when they would be difficult to enforce because the evidence of the violation is hidden. Surgery on the upper part of the roof of the mouths of Bulldogs, done to relieve respiratory problems that cause the dog to snort, is not permitted, but it is commonly done. There is a surgery done to the muscles of the tails of Danes that prevents them from holding the tail high above the back, considered a fault. It's illegal under the rules but many people have had it done on their dogs.

Then there are the unwritten rules, like wearing proper show attire. Nothing says you have to wear a sport coat, suit, or a dress in the show ring, but pretty much everybody does. These are the kinds of rules you have to learn by going to the shows and observing what is going on.

When I found out about all this, I thought it was unique to the show world. But I realized there are plenty of instances in all areas of life when people either think the rules don't apply to them, or when there are rules that people break without consequences, or when there are clear but unwritten rules that you have to learn the hard way. Maybe in this respect the show world is more a microcosm of human behavior than an aberration.

The day after we set up Kunga's crate in the grooming area and nearly got thrown out by walking into an empty ring, we arrived early for the first day of the show. I was breathless with nerves and Kunga was on his toes, feeling my excitement but not sure what he could do about it. Danes often show early in the day because they're among the breeds—such as Dobermans, Viszlas, and Weimeraners—that show people say "have no hair." They mean that these short-coated breeds are easy to groom. We just wash the dog, trim its nails, and cut off its whiskers and eyebrow hairs (Kunga hates that part), and we're ready to go. The Poodle, Samoyed, Pekingese, and Pomeranian handlers open the grooming areas and close them down at night: those coats require unbelievable amounts of attention. I used to think the Puli and Komondor owners had it great: their dogs grow long hair into matted dreadlocks that are not supposed to be brushed. That's until I learned that of course the coats still have to be clean for show, and it can take days for them to dry. These long-haired dogs often are shown later in the day as a concession to their poor handlers who would otherwise have to start grooming them in the middle of the night.

I put Kunga in his crate and went to change clothes. Dog shows in the U.S. are surprisingly formal: the judges and all the handlers get dressed up even at tiny local shows. The men wear suits or sports coats (ties often come off at outdoor events in the summer) and the women are in skirts, suits, or other equally dressy attire. You can spot the amateurs and newbies at these events; they're the ones who are wearing jeans or sweatshirts.

Once I was in my show outfit, I went to the ring area to collect my armband with Kunga's show number. You get this piece of paper from the ring steward, the official who is assisting the judge with organizing and announcing the classes. She looks you up and checks off your dog's name as she gives you the armband; now your dog is officially present for the competition. You secure your number with twin rubber bands around your left arm, and show it to the steward when you enter the ring. When judging is finished, the judge and steward take down the armband numbers of the winners.

With my armband attached, I went to the vendor section of the show building to buy some bait. Almost all shows have an area set aside for a full shopping experience. You can buy leashes, collars, shampoos, toys, crates, jewelry, and T-shirts at even the smallest shows. The bigger shows offer even more choices of vendors, where you can get specialty grooming coats, photos, or painted portraits of your dog.

I wandered through the vendors until I found one selling bait in little individual packets, bought some to use in the ring, and picked up a packet for Carol, who'd asked me to get some extra for her. To my dismay, it was frozen solid! I ran back to the grooming area and handed Carol her share.

"It's frozen, what are we going to do?" I asked.

"Oh, no problem," Carol replied, and promptly tucked the packet of frozen bait into her bra to let it thaw out.

Yow! I couldn't quite bring myself to do this. Instead I put my packet under my arm and began walking around to distract myself from how really uncomfortable it was to have frozen meat next to my skin.

As I walked out onto the arena floor wincing from a cold armpit, a crackling from loudspeakers that was some sort of incomprehensible announcement startled me. Everyone else seemed to understand it, though, and silence—at least as much as possible with over a thousand dogs around—fell over the arena. All eyes turned toward the stands, where an American flag hung in the bleachers. The national anthem began playing over the loudspeakers.

This is a standard part of the culture of dog shows: before every show the anthem is either played or sung, and people salute the flag with varying amounts of attention and fervency. Even the famous Westminster Kennel Club show starts with the national anthem and a video rendering of a billowing flag on the giant overhead monitors. This can be either pretty rote or extremely emotional. Often the anthem is a pre-recorded tape that crackles and pops like an old LP. But I remember a show in Rapid City, SD, where an active-duty serviceman stood in a spotlight before the flag, dressed in camouflage fatigues, and sang the anthem *a cappella* in a compelling tenor that had the full attention of the entire show. Even the blow driers were silenced for those few moments. I don't think there was a dry eye in the crowd.

Once the anthem was over, I consulted the Judging Program to be certain I had the correct ring time. This program arrives in your mail about a week before the show, and is a complete guide to the time each breed of dog will show, which ring they'll be in, the name of the judge, and the number of other class dogs and bitches as well as the number of "specials" for the breed class. Specials are dogs that have already earned their AKC championships and don't compete at the lower level classes. They only enter the ring during the last class, for "Best of Breed."

The classes are divided by gender: all the boys are judged first, then all the girls. (You can imagine why when you remember that none of these dogs are neutered or spayed.) The classes start with the puppies, first 6-9 months old, then 9-12 months. The teenagers are next in the 12-18 month class. The age-related classes are followed by the "Bred by Exhibitor" class, where the handlers are the ones who have bred the dog they're showing, the "American Bred" and "Amateur Owner-Handler" classes. Then come the "Open" classes, which in Danes are shown by color in alphabetical order: black, blue, brindle, fawn, harlequin, and mantle. Since fawn and brindle are more popular colors, smaller shows might have separate open classes for fawns, brindles, and what they call "AOAC," or "any other acceptable color." This is where Kunga often winds up, among what Dane people call the "color." This is a class for dogs that are blue, black, harlequin, and mantle. There are some judges who don't like "color" dogs. It's a weird kind of bias that I find truly odd.

After all the classes of boys are judged, the winners of each class head into the ring together so the judge can choose "Winner's Dog": this is the dog judged best of all the boys competing in the classes. The Winner's Dog gets points toward his championship based on the number of dogs he has beaten that day. Any show with more than three points at stake is called a "major," and during your quest for a championship, your dog must win at least two majors. This prevents a handler from amassing all 15 required championship points by going to little shows and winning over only a few other dogs. At least twice, under two different judges, your dog has to beat some serious competition.

The Winner's Dog goes out of the ring with a purple ribbon and waits for all the girls to be judged, in the same kinds of classes. The winners of each of those classes enter the ring to try for "Winner's Bitch." The winning bitch then trots out of the ring and finally the big one happens: the Best of Breed class. The specials are brought into the ring first to line up, followed by the Winner's Dog and the Winner's Bitch. The judge must choose which of them will be Best of Breed: the best dog regardless of gender present that day. She also picks Best of Opposite Sex, which is nothing but a nice recognition of the dog that's the best of the opposite sex of the Best of Breed winner. Finally, the judge picks Best of Winners, which means she decides which of the Winner's Dog or Winner's Bitch is the better specimen. Sometimes the judge will pick either the Winner's Dog or Winner's Bitch as the Best of Breed: this is known as a "class dog" winning over a special. It's not done often and can be the subject of great glee by the owner of the class dog, who gets to brag they won "over specials."

At this first show, Kunga was entered in a class for 9-12 month old puppies. The only other dog in the class was a harlequin with a professional handler. The steward called the class into the ring in "catalog order," meaning from lowest number to highest: "Great Danes, 9-12 months: Number 7, Number 35!" Uh-oh, my number was called first! I checked Kunga to make sure he didn't have drool spilling out of his lips, whispered "come on, big boy," and pranced into the ring. I trotted Kunga to the same place we started in Carol's handling class, about halfway around. I looked back to gauge how much the judge was impressed by my gorgeous blue dog, only to see the steward sternly gesturing for me to come back since I'd missed the proper place to start. I had to trot Kunga back, my face red in humiliation, to the correct place, and stack him up. How embarrassing! There I stood, sweating, waiting for the judge to examine the dog. Instead, she immediately asked us to move the dogs around the ring, which confused me since in the practice classes we didn't do that until after examination. This was when I learned that no two judges are alike in what they want, so I'd better pay attention.

Kunga behaved reasonably well. His tail was wagging full time, making it clear he was enjoying himself. After she'd had the chance to put her hands on Kunga, the judge ordered us to do the down and back on the diagonal. Kunga shook his head with puppy impatience, but didn't try to pull me around. The next thing the judge asked was that we trot all the way around the ring and end up behind the other dog in the class, where we waited until that dog had gone through the same process. By the time the second dog finished, I had Kunga stacked nicely—still wagging his tail—for the judge to see. She looked at the two dogs from across the ring and pointed to the one behind us.

"One," she said, then pointed at Kunga and said "two." In about three and a half minutes we'd lost our first class.

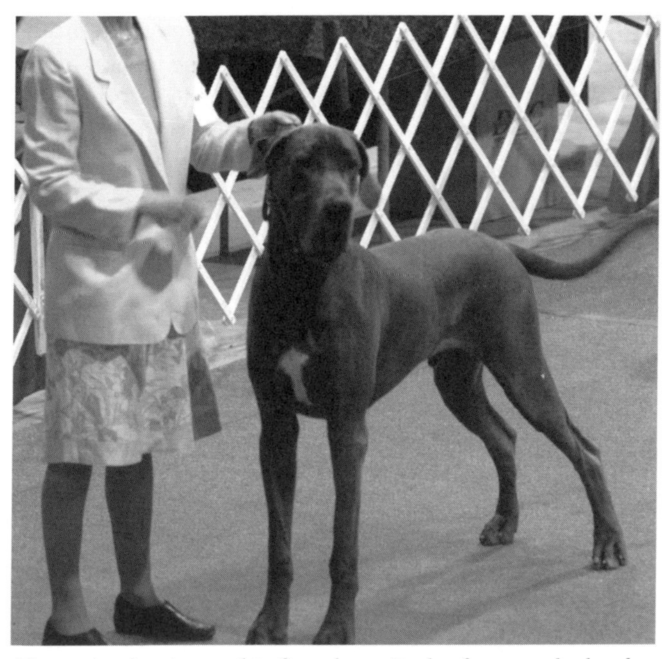

Kunga in the ring at his first show. Both of us are clueless but having fun.

But…Kunga had behaved well, and I hadn't tripped and fallen in the ring, something that happens with distressing frequency to novice competitors. Though I'd made some obvious and ridiculous handling errors, I was pumped with adrenaline, excited by the competition. Kunga was popping with his own joy and understanding that something fun was going on, hopping from one front foot to the other and trying to jump up to lick my face while the judge was taking our number for the records. We jogged out of the ring with a red, second-place ribbon that I still have and cherish.

My friends and mentors gathered around. "You should have won," they all said. "He was great. He was much prettier than the winner."

This is what friends are for: to encourage you, to loyally support you, and to tell you—whether true or not—that for sure you have the better dog. I probably lost the class for Kunga within the first few seconds when I made it clear I didn't know how to handle him or follow directions. But despite the loss and my ineptitude, the hook was set, and I was already looking forward to the next time I could get Kunga into the ring.

CHAPTER 4
Losing

Losing sucks. Everyone hates losing. But you do an awful lot of it when you're showing your dog. In fact, the standard advice to every dog show beginner is: if you can't stand losing, get out, because you'll lose many more times than you'll win.

I brought Kunga home as a pet and had no expectations about him as a show dog, which made me less invested in him as a winner. When I went to our first show in Denver, I didn't think he'd win anything, and in fact he didn't.

Our second show was in Scottsbluff, Nebraska, and I had no greater expectations for that event than I did for the first time around. I figured it was a nice small show where I could get some experience handling so I would not look so inept down the road. My stepdaughter came along to give me a hand with moving all the show equipment and a large dog. I was grateful for the help, since the amount of stuff you lug around to shows is staggering. It's like traveling with a toddler, with lots of specialized gear. When I travel to shows, I pack not only Kunga's crate, but also a pad and fleece for the inside; a blanket to cover the outside of the crate to provide a sense of security and some warmth; the dog bowl; food;

toys; a grooming bag; a dog bed for the hotel room; Kunga's favorite red blanket; special treats; paper towels; poop bags; and show clothes and shoes for me. I get one small tote bag for all my stuff.

When I got set up at the show grounds on the first morning of the show, Kunga didn't like the crate in the open grooming area of the show and wouldn't go into it without a fight. He was mesmerized by the other dogs and wouldn't pay attention to me as I tried to get him ready for the class. I couldn't even get him to walk around the grounds without him hauling on the leash, much less practice stacking him. I had a very bad feeling about taking him into the ring at all.

Then, surprise! Kunga took Winner's Dog on the first day of the show. I was so dazed and pleased I had to call Cindy, his breeder, to brag about this very first win. Though he earned only one point because there were so few dogs competing that day, I think I went on about it to everyone I knew for several weeks afterward. I could hardly believe my Dane had actually started on the long road to a championship. After this one measly point, I suddenly became ambitious: maybe Kunga could be a famous, winning stud dog, going to Westminster or the Eukanuba championships and getting on TV! (Well, I could dream, couldn't I?)

That first win spoiled me for losing. It made the next day of the show bitter, when under a different judge Kunga lost to my friend Loren's dog. For the first time, I lost when I thought I could win, and it was not nice at all.

There are many reasons to enter a dog in a show, and it's not always for a win. Some people do it to build the entry numbers so that there is a "major" for the other dogs; some do it for handling practice, even if they don't expect their dog is good enough to win. In these cases, people expect to lose and have no misery when that happens. But if you take your dog into the ring believing you can win, it's pretty awful when you don't. Most of us know our dog's faults—we'd be nuts if we didn't assess the dog before deciding to show—but still believe these faults are fewer than those of the other dogs in the ring. So when we lose it's a real blow.

I've worried about whether losing will change my relationship with Kunga. At first when he lost I was disappointed, and when he misbehaved and lost, I got angry.

Our relationship as owner and dog was truly tested as we continued to show and lose. One of these trying times occurred soon after Kunga's first win, at a show in Laramie, WY. Wyoming is not an especially warm place in May. The sky was growling with clouds and it rained on and off all weekend the first time I went to this show. This puts everyone in a nasty mood, since it's hard to move clean, groomed dogs from the grooming area to the show rings in other buildings without getting muddy, wind-blown or soaked. I even helped carry a 60-pound Bearded Collie with long, flowing white and gray hair over a muddy pathway so the handler wouldn't have to re-groom the dog all over again at the ring!

The first day of showing, Kunga won his class and I found myself in the Winner's Dog ring with my friend Kathryn, who was showing a Dane for someone else. When she won, I was disappointed, but not too upset. On Saturdays, losing is a bit easier. There's always Sunday's show to make up for it. Shows are almost always at least two days, with different judges on each day.

But on Sunday, something must have gotten to Kunga, because he was a lunatic on a leash. He wouldn't settle down before the class, and since it was raining I didn't have the option of taking him for a long walk to settle him down. When we danced into the ring with him nearly turning circles around me, I knew things were going to be bad. And they were—Kunga wouldn't stack properly, he wouldn't be still during examination, he wouldn't even trot down and back to the end of the ring without flinging his legs out everywhere and turning to look at the people outside the ring. He lost, of course, but we were lucky not to be dismissed for bad behavior. My friend Carol watched the class, and asked, "Were you doing the can-can in there?!?" as we came out.

I was humiliated, and angry with Kunga, who didn't know that he had done anything wrong. My only thought was to pack up and get back home as soon as possible, preferably without anyone seeing us. I pushed him into the car and stomped off to get the remainder of the show equipment, including the crate, which I had to drag across mud-spattered wood planks. By the time I got back to the car, there was a young man smiling at Kunga and pointing to him through the windows. As I came up, I recognized the guy as someone who'd recently lost his old dog to disease, and had come to the dog show to research breeds to see what kind of dog he should get next.

This is a great idea, by the way. Unless they're about to go into the ring, nearly everybody at a show is happy to have you pet their dog and will tell you more than you could possibly need to know about the breed. Just don't ask if you or your sticky-fingered child can pet the dog before it has finished showing.

The guy had fallen in love with Kunga on Saturday, and was back with his girlfriend to show her what he looked like. He'd searched the entire show grounds and the parking lot until he found us. I was still upset at our loss but couldn't pass up the opportunity to use this guy's muscle to help me get my crate onto the top of my car. I offered to get Kunga out and let them pet him if they'd give me a hand, which the man gladly did. Then I put a lead on Kunga's collar and he jumped out of the back seat, shimmying with pleasure. He leaned on the man as he accepted the petting and hugging and scratching, turning in circles with excitement. The guy was nearly out of his mind in dog love.

"Isn't he just the perfect dog?" he asked his girlfriend.

And just like that, my anger evaporated. In fact, I do think Kunga's the perfect dog. He is my lovely blue boy and I can't get enough of him. He sleeps in our room at night and stretches out at my feet when I work at my computer, and he gives little leaps of joy whenever I come near him. So how could I be so pissed off at him? Just because for one 3-minute stretch he found it hard to contain his general joie de vivre? I realized the expectation of winning a show could actually undo my whole relationship with him if I let winning become more than just some fortuitous thing that happens every once in a while. Losing shouldn't make you angry at your dog. I stepped back as the young guy tried to convince his less-than-enthusiastic girlfriend that a giant Dane would make a perfect pet, and realized how incredibly lucky I was just to have Kunga in my life, win or lose.

My big blue buddy and me.

It's difficult to have an ordinary connection with your dog when you show. Showing is performing, and good performance takes practice, so you have a lot of training to do with the dog. They'd generally rather play around, and if you let this happen you won't be able to show effectively. Kunga used to lean over and lick my face as I tried to stack him in the ring. This always drew a big "awwww" from the onlookers, but in fact it's a form of passive resistance. He was asking nicely if we could do something other than this right now. I've had to learn to be more businesslike in the ring with him; he has to know that's his work time, not time for play. This can be fun or frustrating, depending on the owner's attitude and how much of her ego gets wrapped up in the dog's behavior and success. Losing also tests the relationship. What happens when your dog doesn't win much?

A relative of mine had a Standard Schnauzer that she showed years ago. She believed that her wonderful dog would be a winner, but soon found that he wasn't really up to snuff. He also hated the show ring, hated being with a handler and away from home. My relative didn't care about the ribbons, so she retired the dog without a championship. But she remembers him with great fondness. Unlike for many of us, the losing didn't make any difference to her.

Others aren't so balanced. I've seen owners so unhappy with a loss they slam the dog crate door closed on a bewildered dog, who probably didn't understand what the fuss was about. At one show I met a spectator who was deliriously happy with the little Sheltie by her side, fussing and cooing so much I had to stop and ask about the dog. It turned out that the woman was the brand-new owner of the Sheltie, having just acquired her from her frustrated former owner. The dog had showed badly for over a year, and was so disappointing in the ring that day that her owner had given her away on the spot to the first person who came by and admired the dog!

Breeders who show can be a little colder-eyed about their animals than an ordinary pet owner. They are working to produce quality dogs that will win and continue to build the prestige of their kennel. Among the happiest winning handlers I've seen have been those in the bred-by class, exhibiting dogs who they have bred, raised and trained and then handled themselves in the show ring. But the breeders also know that there are some dogs that are just not going to be up to snuff, who will never finish their championships. While many breeders will keep those dogs as beloved pets, some will find other homes for them as soon as they know they will never earn a championship. Until I met that woman with her Sheltie, though, I'd never heard of one giving away a dog in a fit of pique at losing. The dog was lucky to have landed with someone who obviously adored her and was already at the vendor stands buying dog dishes, the best food, a comfy bed, and toys.

In the spring after his first birthday, Kunga began to shed his puppy coat. In any Dane this is unsightly, but in the dark-colored blue and black Danes, it can be truly awful. Kunga turned a dusty brown color as the old fur died. The worst part was that the fur that refused to fall out, clinging to him in hideous patches.

At least I had something new to blame (other than my inexperienced handling) as we continued our string of losses. After Laramie, we traveled all over Colorado to shows, losing each time. Sometimes we'd lose in a class, sometimes Kunga would win a class but then lose in the Winner's Dog ring. Once or twice he was Reserve Winner's Dog, a second-place finish that some show people call "first loser." It gets you no points and can be frustrating. In fact, I saw someone with a t-shirt that sold out at the Great Dane nationals. Over the picture of a Dane's head, it said "AFR." Every show person could decipher that one as "Another F*ing Reserve." It's good when you can joke about it.

You can do a lot of losing while "winning" the popular vote. There are almost always a few people ringside who don't know anything about your breed, but are fascinated by the dogs. Some have pet dogs of the same breed and are wondering whether their dog could do this fancy prancing around to win ribbons. Others just wander from ring to ring, stopping when a breed catches their eye. I remember standing outside a ring as the Winner's Bitch class was being judged, listening to a little girl talking to her mother. The mother had asked someone nearby about the colors of the dogs in the ring, but must have misheard when told they were fawn. When her daughter pointed and said that yellow one was her favorite, the mother replied knowingly, "That one's called a blonde, dear."

All these onlookers have their opinions about which dog should win the classes. Often, they're partial to Kunga. Though there can be a dozen other people with Danes standing around, many people approach us to talk. Maybe it's his natural ears, or his unusual color, but he certainly gets a lot of attention ringside, both from other dog show people and from those who know nothing about the breed. At one show, I had crowd support from security guards, an old lady in a motor chair, and a pack of Girl Scouts who were volunteer pooper-scoopers at the show grounds. They all cheered when Kunga went around the ring, even when he was the only one in the class. I've had people ask if Kunga has sired puppies. I've even had one person ask if he was for sale. (Sorry, no way.) Too bad the audience doesn't get a vote for Winner's Dog, like on the TV show "American Idol." However, the positive feedback outside the ring is one of the things that makes losing in the ring a little more bearable.

Considering how painful it is to lose, I was amazed to discover that there is a widespread practice in the dog show world of trying to lose. It's called, ungrammatically, "laying down" on your dog, and it happens when a handler wants to give away his points to a dog of the opposite gender. Sometimes only one gender of a breed (say, for example, the dogs) has a major at a show, while there are not enough entries in the other gender (in this case, the bitches) for a major win. Then the Winner's Bitch could also earn a major by beating the Winner's Dog for Best of Winners. The Winner's Dog doesn't lose any points by this; the bitch just gets more points than she would have if she only beat all the girls. Experienced handlers know this, and will often make a bid for the better-pointed dog to lose the Best of Winners class.

There are some pretty standard formulas for this. Either just before going into the ring, or in a whispered conversation as everyone is lining up, the lower-pointed handler will mention how very much his animal needs these points. If the higher pointed handler is willing to allow the other to win, they will do their best to see that their dog doesn't win the Best of Winners. After all, their dog doesn't lose any points by doing so, though of course it would mean losing not only the Best of Winners, but also a chance to beat those specials (the champions) for Best of Breed. There are no rules against this—how you show your dog in the ring is up to you.

How does the handler do this? They show poorly. Some will simply stroll into the ring and not even make an effort to stack their dog. Others will stack the dog carelessly, or not use bait to get the best expression of the dog. The handler can move the dog badly, by either going too quickly or too slowly, or even pulling the head around slightly with the lead or with bait so that the dog's stride is crabbed sideways instead of correct. These tricks can be risky. Some judges will take offense that an exhibitor is clearly not trying in their class, and though they will rarely give the dog the win out of spite, an insulted judge will remember that handler for a good long while.

Some handlers will lay down on their dogs as a favor to the other handler if they don't think their own dog can win the breed. Others won't do this at all. Either is considered acceptable in the show world, as long as you are honest about your intentions. One friend of mine needed a major for her dog to finish his championship, but got only two points for Winner's Dog. The show was a 3-point major for the bitches, however, so she sidled up to the Winner's Bitch handler as they walked into the ring and mentioned how her dog really needed the major.

"Oh, no problem," replied the bitch's handler. "I understand what you need, don't worry." This is recognized code for an agreement to lay down on the bitch, but the handler didn't follow through. Instead, she made a major effort to show the bitch and hoped to take the breed. My friend was furious, not because the bitch's handler eventually won Best of Winners (depriving her dog of the major), but because there had been a pretty clear understanding that it wouldn't go that way. My friend won't forget that other handler, and you can be sure that she will in turn tell her friends about the betrayal. This kind of thing gets around the dog world fast. That handler will find it hard to get any one else to lay down on their dog for her in the future.

Show people invest a lot of money in their dogs (more on that later) and on all the accoutrements of showing. More importantly, they invest a lot of ego in whether the dog wins or loses. Unfortunately, this can lead to a lot of bad behavior. At one recent show, I heard a famous handler—furious at what he thought had been undue influence on the judge—swear at the winner's owner and her handler in a loud voice and in front of all the other exhibitors standing ringside, including a 13 year old junior handler standing nearby. This is considered unacceptable behavior in the show world. It's a place of old-fashioned values, and people care about decorum. It may be an intensely political place, where favors are traded and unfair advantage is gained depending on who handles a dog, but these things are discussed sotto voce, in gossip over dinner or in the grooming areas. A deliberate display of poor sportsmanship when losing is not only bad form, it can get you fined or suspended if the AKC representative or show committee hears of it. You learn to take your losses with a smile, and always congratulate the winner whether you think you were robbed or not.

I did a lot of congratulating and not much winning that first summer with Kunga. After one of our many losses, I called home to tell my husband that once again we'd driven a long way and paid good money to lose.

"Really?" he asked. "Is Kunga upset?"

My husband is a Zen priest and a very wise man. He was reminding me that the dog has no idea what winning or losing means. Kunga only knows if I am happy or sad after running around the ring for a few minutes, and is clueless what he might have done or not done to cause either state. I've made it a practice ever since that day to lean over Kunga at the end of every single class, no matter what his placement in it, and give him a big hug. I tell him I love him. He's happy no matter what color ribbon we get.

CHAPTER 5
Professional Handlers, Judges, and Politics

In May 2009, our breed club put on its annual "specialty" show, a double show only for Great Danes. It was a major, drawing dogs from across the west to compete, including a top twenty Great Dane. I was thrilled to compete with Kunga in his first specialty, but had one problem: I had a business commitment that meant I had to leave after the morning show. Either I had to take Kunga home after the morning, or leave him with someone else to handle in the second show. It would be his first experience in the ring with a professional handler or anyone other than me.

I was amazed at the size of the professional handling industry when I first began to show. At first I couldn't believe that handling was enough of a specialized talent that people could actually make a living doing it. After a few times in the ring I learned better: a professional, experienced handler can make a good dog look terrific and can help to gloss over a mediocre dog's faults. An inept handler can make even a superstar dog look bad. For that reason, it's unusual to see an owner handling a "special," one of the dogs that competes after earning his or her championship. There are even some breeds, like German Shepherds, where professionals take in most of the dogs in the lower level classes, because they are difficult dogs to show well.

When the time came that I couldn't show my own boy at that specialty, I decided that Carol's husband Don, a professional handler like Carol, could do a good job. Don is quieter and more soft-spoken than Carol, but has a keen competitive instinct. Though he hasn't been showing long, he has a remarkable record of wins, and he seems to have a natural feel for dogs. Judges like him. He's a decent-looking guy with fashionably gelled hair, he's polite, and he wears a suit well. Kunga and Don had spent time together in handling classes and seemed to have a bond. Carol and Don also agreed to keep Kunga all weekend while I was away and show him in the two shows that followed our club specialty. That helped me a lot since Kunga, as an intact male, isn't accepted at most commercial kennels.

I showed Kunga in the morning specialty and didn't win anything. Reluctantly, I left him with Don and headed out for my business meeting. I was out of cell phone range all weekend, but hurried to check messages as soon as I could when I was on the way home. To my astonishment, I found out that Kunga had gone Winner's Dog in the afternoon specialty for his first 3-point major! Though I was thrilled to hear of the win, I had mixed emotions about it. I was sad that I hadn't been there to see it, and disappointed that I hadn't been able to do it myself.

There's the strange conundrum for the amateur owner-handler: you have fun showing, but you may not do it as well as a professional can or have the "pull" with the judge that some handlers have. I love trotting proudly into the ring with Kunga and showing him off to the judge and onlookers. But I also wanted him to be a champion, and it was a bit galling that he could have a better chance at that with a professional handler than with me. It's a war between ego and ambition that I've never really resolved. When Kunga won that first major, I realized he might actually be a winning dog, and that was the match that lit my aspiration to have Kunga go all the way to a championship. Admittedly, at that point he had only 4 points out of the necessary 15, but I began to believe in his possibility as a winner.

Don Volleberg preparing a young Rotteweiler to show.

Just as my desire to show grew, I began to notice how many professionals I competed against. Carol and Don are not my only friends who handle other people's dogs. Many of the members of the Dane club are also professionals, though not all make a living at it. Carol runs a boarding and training facility, for example, and Don has his own business as well. Kathryn has a day job but also shows Danes, Samoyeds, and other breeds on the weekends. My friend Craig shows his own Danes, but also handles for other people in addition to running his own kennel and training business. (Though he'll have to stop showing Danes for other people: he's now a provisional judge in Danes, which means he can't handle any dogs but his own professionally anymore.)

Who are all these people? Should you consider turning your dog over to a professional to be shown? As I spent more time at shows, I learned that the handlers come from all kinds of backgrounds and vary greatly in their expertise.

At a show in Topeka, I sat in the stands to watch the Group judging for sporting dogs. These are the winners of their breed classes who are competing for a Group win or top four finish and have hopes of making the Best in Show class. I found a seat next to an older woman who was following the action quite closely, and who reserved her applause for the black Cocker Spaniel when it came up for individual examination.

"Is that your dog?" I asked.

"No," she said, "That's my son handling him. He's a professional handler."

She told me Jeff's story. He had been a shy, introverted boy. In an attempt to bring him out of his shell, his parents bought him a dog as a companion, a Cocker Spaniel puppy. Jeff delighted in the dog and spent hours grooming and training the little guy. Even though he was a child, he was consumed by that belief that his dog could be a champion in the show ring. His parents indulged him by bringing him to some shows to watch, and eventually he entered his dog himself. There was no "Junior Handler" system then (a kind of minor league of handling for kids 18 and under), but Jeff worked hard and learned about grooming, stacking, and moving his dog. He went to work for a kennel where he could begin to pick up the finer points of the sport. Today, Jeff Wright is among the best-known Cocker Spaniel handlers in the nation.

People become handlers through different routes. Many come from show families—where a parent enjoys showing or breeding dogs—and learn at home how to present the breed. My friend Lisa Goodman started that way. Her mother showed Samoyeds. Lisa got so sick of shows as a teenager that she eventually pitched a fit and swore she'd never go to another dog show in her life. The show world doesn't let go so easily, though, and soon she was breeding and showing her own Pomeranians. She quit her day job in 2009 and began her business as a full-time handler of toy breeds. Her only explanation for her return to showing? "I just love the dogs," she says.

That's a must for handlers. While you can make a living, and sometimes a very good one, it's not generally very lucrative to handle dogs, and it's both time-consuming as well as physically demanding. It's a point of pride for many professionals that their dogs are always cared for first, before they take care of themselves. Lisa once drove 27 Pomeranians to the national specialty, and for the entire trip she had to be sure that every one of them was fed, cleaned, and taken for what show people euphemistically call "exercise" (peeing and pooping) before she could eat or do her own laundry.

At each show the handler puts together the set-up of crates, grooming table, blow driers, grooming tools, and assorted pads, blankets, and leashes. You see people dragging carts with teetering piles of equipment through the grooming area on the day before the show. Smaller crates come assembled, but larger crates have to be put together from assorted parts, like a puzzle. Each dog has to be bathed and groomed for every show; that's on top of the time the dogs require for feeding and exercise. I almost never see a professional handler sitting down at a show. If they're not grooming or exercising, they're standing ringside or running around inside the ring showing their dogs. This is tough on the body. One famous handler has had both hips replaced and wears special shoes to reduce the impact on his joints as he shows. It's a demanding and tiring way to make a living.

Of course, it's easier for the big-name handlers in the sport, since many have assistants to do some of the grunt work. These are the pros who travel in immense RVs and arrive at shows with 20 or more dogs in tow. Some of them are independently wealthy or have indulgent (rich) spouses, but most are able to travel in style because they're extremely good at showing dogs. The people who own the great show dogs also often have a great deal of money. They can afford to buy into the best bloodlines and can pay to have the dog developed by top handlers.

Some of these pros get out of touch with why they started in the first place—love for the dogs. If you decide you want to turn your dog over to a handler rather than showing yourself, you should spend some time researching who would be the best person for you and your dog.

When I asked one of my friends why she chose her particular professional, she described watching many different handlers carefully at shows for months. Of course she saw them performing in the ring, but she also observed them at their grooming areas, when they were out of the spotlight, when almost no one was paying attention. There, she saw handlers with tempers, shouting at assistants and yanking the collars of the dogs, speaking roughly to them. Eventually she chose her handler, the well-known Michael Brantley, because she never saw him treat a dog badly, whether in the ring or out of it.

Michael is hugely liked and respected in the show world, a reputation he has earned in over 45 years of showing dogs. He started by showing Chow Chows with his parents, and began handling dogs for other people from the time he was 18 years old. Now he is an all-breed handler with Best in Show titles too numerous for him to remember. Though he travels comfortably in a big rig, he must travel often. He is on the road for all but about three to four weeks per year, caring for the dogs, overseeing his assistants, keeping entries and records current, and of course showing, showing, showing. It helps that his wife, Linda, a handler herself, both understands his life and is able to sometimes travel with him. She is also the manager of their boarding kennel at home, though, so their time together is limited.

Other well-known handlers choose a different route, without the big rigs and the assistants. Mari Lynn Davisson is a well-known Dane handler who also takes on other breeds like Rottweilers and Bulldogs. Mari Lynn didn't come from a show family. She started out with a Rottweiler—a family pet—while she was living in England. She learned to show in the more casual, family atmosphere of the English show, where there aren't many professional handlers and people don't dress in suits to go into the ring. Dog shows in England are a fun day out, where the kids romp around as the parents get their dogs groomed for the ring. Handling is different there, too, since the dogs are walked into a natural stance and are rarely hand-stacked as required in America. Championships are harder to get, however: your dog must compete in an open class with all other dogs, including existing champions, and cannot get a "CC" (points toward a championship) unless they are one of the overall winners.

Mari Lynn Davisson in the ring with a Rottweiler "special."

When Mari Lynn moved back to the United States, she continued to show Rottweilers as she learned the very different etiquette of the American show ring. For about four years, she was a schoolteacher full time and showed dogs on the weekends. She was soon handling friends' dogs, and doing very well at it. Someone asked if she'd consider handling a Dane special, and soon she had a number of Danes to bring to the shows. She fell in love with the breed, and began to own and breed them herself. Eventually, she decided that handling was her real life mission, and when she and her husband moved to Arizona, she decided to try to make a living at it full time.

She has been very successful showing dogs throughout the western U.S. and doing well at the Great Dane Nationals, where one of her girls took Winner's Bitch in 2009. She is a trim, strong woman with an unassuming manner. She has chosen to pursue her handling career without hiring assistants. This limits her income, since she must groom, exercise, and show every single animal she brings to the shows by herself, or ask for help from others at ringside. She could take on more dogs if she hired assistants, but she feels strongly that she is promising each client her personal attention to their dog. "They don't pay me to have someone else take their dog into the ring," she says.

Whether big-time or small scale, though, the life of a professional handler is lived mostly on the road. They are competing almost every weekend of the year, all over a region or even, for some, all over the country. They live out of motels or RVs or motor trailers, find laundromats along the way, and eat a lot of junk food because you can drive through the fast-food places without having to worry about leaving your dogs alone in a hotel room and it takes no preparation time. It's hard to organize your life this way. Lisa manages because her mother (who still breeds Samoyeds) moved in with her and takes care of a lot of the routine things required to keep a house going such as paying bills, cleaning the kennel, and coordinating the schedules of the owners, shows, and dogs. Other people, like Mari Lynn, have supportive spouses. My friends Carol and Don both handle professionally, so they have each other to rely upon. But it's a hard life, and one that may not include much socializing. Anyone who's on the road seven weeks out of eight is going to have a hard time maintaining a relationship.

While most professionals win because they handle top dogs and are highly skilled, an unfortunate truth is that they sometimes have an edge in the ring simply because they're known to the judge. I don't mean they have close personal relationships, though that can be the case. It's just that a handler showing 45 weeks a year is likely to run into the same judges frequently as they crisscross the country. If a familiar face comes into the ring, the judge wouldn't be human if she didn't take an extra look at the dog at the other end of the leash. "Sad, but true," Lisa tells me, that the professionals have this advantage over owner-handlers like me. The pros often know a judge's preferences and biases so well that they know whether or not to enter a particular dog in a class with a specific judge. If they're good, the pros will avoid bringing a type that the judge won't like, and the judges learn that this handler is likely to bring only a good dog that the judge is inclined to appreciate into the ring. That, too, earns the professionals an extra look that an amateur won't get. Michael Brantley started out with Chows, and he points out that he has spent so long in the breed that he taught some of the current judges lessons on breed type. It would be almost inhuman if a judge he was showing to didn't at least give a dog with Michael at the other end of the leash a good hard look.

This is an ongoing battle in the show world. Owner-handlers complain about judges that won't put their dogs in the winner's spot because some Famous Handler is in the ring with an inferior dog but a better-known face. I think that definitely does happen. Other times, though, we owners aren't seeing the myriad ways in which the pros are doing a better job of presenting their dogs.

When Kunga goes into the ring with me, we both have a hard time giving up our usual relationship. Although Kunga's not a bad dog, there are behaviors that I let him get away with just because I think he's adorable or he makes me laugh with what he's doing. Kunga takes that belief in my indulgence into the ring, and that sometimes makes it hard for me to get him to show well. By contrast, if Don is handling, the energy changes. Don likes Kunga a lot, but he doesn't let him get away with a sloppy stack or with goofing off in the ring. Don also has years more experience than me, can stack Kunga quicker than I can, and knows better how to correct his head during movement than I do.

These are the advantages the professionals often have over amateurs: they pay attention to small details, they move crisply and precisely, they often know what a judge likes and they try to get the dog to present that aspect to her. For example, if a judge tends to focus on a proper topline (the line of the back from neck to tail), a good handler will be sure to stroke the dog slowly and deliberately along his back to draw the judge's attention to it. Handlers often stare intently at the best part of the dog they're showing, or touch the dog there, to be sure the judge at least notices that part. Watch the Westminster or Eukanuba shows on TV some time and see the handlers with the long-coated breeds wield those combs and brushes after the judge has examined their dogs. This is not frivolous: they're drawing attention to the wonderful coat as they get the dog ready to do its movement. Though there's a simmering resentment from owner-handlers when we get beaten by the professionals, we don't always acknowledge that someone else could just be doing a better job in the ring.

That said, there are also some pretty nasty professional handlers out there who do what they have to in order to win. At one show, I trotted Kunga into the ring first and began to stack him up in the middle of the mat. I was just finishing with his back legs when I noticed that the professional handler behind me had taken advantage of the fact that we were not at the front edge of the mat nearest the judge, and had stacked his dog so that he obscured a lot of Kunga's back end. From where the judge stood, he would only be able to see Kunga's front, with the rest hidden behind the next dog in line! I quickly walked Kunga forward a few steps out of his stack and put him at the front edge of the mat to re-stack him. By then, though, Kunga was antsy and confused, and it took me a while to get him back into the correct position. While he was still dancing around the judge asked us all to begin moving around the ring together. Since I was in the front of the line, I had to stand up quickly and get Kunga's collar set and ready to move, which flustered me a bit. I could see the little satisfied smirk on the face of the handler behind me as I got ready. He had succeeded in getting both Kunga and I uncomfortable and off balance, and gave his dog a better chance of winning. I was vengefully pleased when Kunga won the class anyway.

These kinds of mean little tricks abound, and are mostly played by professionals, even against each other. Some handlers will move too close to the dog in front when they stack, which invariably makes the front dog unhappy. Some will not wait for you to get ready when the time comes to move around the ring and will leave you flat-footed, holding up the line of moving dogs while the judge frowns. Some handlers toss bait ahead of their dogs to get their attention, without regard to the effect this has on the other dogs in line that might be startled or try to go after a thrown piece of food.

Even really egregious handler misbehavior is hard to stop through official channels. The AKC, ostensibly in charge of discipline, is fairly remote from the everyday show ring, and it's difficult to get the organization to take action. The only way to counteract these things is to be as aggressive but polite in taking up your position and moving in the line along with everyone else. It's part of the learning curve for handling. If you don't like it, you should leave your dog to a professional who knows how to deal with the misconduct.

It seems to me the continuing influx of professionals has changed the dynamic of dog showing. Many of them are trying to earn a living, and they rely on wins in order to get and keep clients. Winning for them is important in a different way than it is for owner-handlers: it's their livelihood. This gives them the incentive to behave badly if it means they take home some points. By no means do all handlers do this, of course; most of them are honorable and fair. I've met many that are welcoming and will give a struggling owner good advice on how to better present their dog. Most depend on their ability to see promise in a young dog and handle it well in order to get ahead in their profession. Yet there are some unscrupulous pros are out there, and to the extent that they abuse their knowledge, they're hurting the sport.

I've jokingly put forward the idea that all the dogs entered for a breed should have each handler randomly assigned to show each dog. I wonder if the same dogs would keep winning this way?

In 2009, the AKC acknowledged amateur owner-handler complaints about professionals in a sort of sideways manner, by instituting a class specifically for us. That gives us the chance to enter a class without professionals to compete against, though the winner still goes on to the Winner's Dog or Bitch class alongside the professionals. So far, however, there are few entrants for this class. In the March 2010 issue of *The Canine Chronicle*, Dr. Bob Smith wondered why that might be. He suggested that there should be an entire track for this AOH class leading to "best AOH in show," or that there be substantial cash prizes to get people to enter.

I think people aren't entering partly because it's a new class, but largely I think it's because we as owners don't want to have our own "advantage" or don't want to look lame. Some judges believe this AOH class to be a matter of judging how well the handler is doing rather than the quality of the dog, sort of like junior handling classes. Some won't seriously consider the dog for Winner's Dog or Winner's Bitch, which is how we get our points. A few amateur owners are showing pet-quality dogs out of ignorance but understandable blind pride, and it's lovely that they get a chance to show. Some enter the AOH class because they have several dogs to show and want to spread them out among classes so they don't compete against each other. But those who believe their dog is the equal of any other in the breed continue to show in the other classes and learn to deal with the ploys of the malicious.

The life of a judge was equally mysterious to me when I started out in showing. When you pay your entry fee, you're essentially paying to get the judge's opinion of your dog. I began to wonder who these experts were and what they got out of it.

At Kunga's first show, the judge stood in front of him and lifted his ears in a caricature of a crop-eared Dane. I had never seen this done before, but then I was new and had no idea what the usual examination procedure was. After I lost, my friend Kelley came up to commiserate with me. Kelley shows a natural-eared bitch, and told me she labeled that ear-lift the "move of death." In her view, the judges who do this don't necessarily know how to judge a natural-eared Dane. It used to be that you couldn't show a Dane in the U.S. unless it had cropped ears, so most of today's judges have grown up only looking at Danes that have that startled, ears-up look. Cropped ears have another advantage, in that they hide part of the skull, which can obscure a slope or other less desirable aspects of the plane of the skull. A natural-eared Dane is a relatively new look for many judges, and some of them just don't like it.

You wouldn't think there could be huge differences of opinion when it comes to judging a dog. There's a written standard, after all, illustrated with pictures as well as an official DVD showing good and bad points of a dog. But most breed standards leave a lot of questions unanswered. In the Dane standard, for example, there are only a few faults that are considered serious (for example, "A ring or hooked tail is a serious fault"), and a few statements about what is preferable (in mantle colored Danes, "whole white collar is preferred"), as well as clear directions for disqualification ("A split nose is a disqualification"). But the standard doesn't state what parts of the dog should be preferred over other parts. Of course, different judges will have different preferences in parts of the dog where the standard gives them some leeway. It is up to the judge to determine if a great overall body structure on a dog without much head trumps another dog with a great head but not very good body structure. If a judge has known preferences and is consistent in her judging, handlers learn to take the type of dog to her that she prefers.

Choosing whether to show to a particular judge is a sport in itself in the dog world. Everyone I know keeps a list of the judges they've shown to, with a note of whether the judge liked their dog or a similar dog. Even I have something that rudimentary; other handlers go much further than this in evaluating a judge. First, they find out if the judge is a breed judge or someone who only qualified later in the breed they're planning to show. The handler will also check the AKC and other web sites like www.infodog.com to find out more about each judge, such as whether she consistently likes or dislikes puppies for winners, or if she favors exhibitors from the bred-by classes or will only choose winners from the Open division. Those who have all been around for a while are likely to know something about those winning dogs, and can tell from who won whether the judge likes a better coat or better structure or better movement.

The *Great Dane Review* has a place on its web site which lists many of the judges approved for Danes, together with their answers to a questionnaire that asks where they're from, what breed they started with, who their mentors were, and what they look for and what they dislike in dogs that come before them. This can be a bit helpful, since judges will sometimes say they think the head is most important, or that movement is the paramount consideration. But the questionnaire doesn't cover some of the insider knowledge that can be gained by actually showing to a judge. It doesn't ask, "Do you hate natural ears? Do you put up professional handlers over amateur owner handlers all the time? Do you consistently like the puppies better than older dogs?" The breed standard prohibits these prejudices, but judges have them nonetheless. I once showed Kunga to a judge only to find out afterward that this judge had NEVER IN HER CAREER put up a black, blue, or mantle Dane as a winner. I just wish I'd known that before I paid my $25 entry and stood around in the hot summer sun to try to win some points under her. I got this valuable information from a professional handler standing ringside, and when I went home I put that judge on my "avoid" list of judges. Live and learn.

Judges are licensed by the AKC (or UKC for their shows) after a lengthy qualifying process. A prospective judge has to have spent time as a steward at licensed shows, judged at matches, passed anatomy exams, and interviewed with an AKC field representative. In order to be licensed to judge their first breed, they must also meet the 12-5-4 eligibility requirements, which requires 12 or more years exhibiting the breed in conformation shows, having bred and raised 5 or more litters of the breed on their premises, and having bred 4 or more champions from those litters. (There are alternative methods of qualifying that are essentially variations on the 12-5-4, but they're similar.)

Becoming a judge isn't cheap. Apart from the years spent either breeding and/or handling dogs, judges have to pay for their own educations, including seminars, breed books, and visits to known breeders. After passing the tests and interviews, they become "provisional" judges and must judge a breed at five different shows (three under the watchful eye of an AKC representative) on their own nickel. The clubs don't pay the judges at this stage in their careers, and often the provisionals will also have to bear the cost of their own round-trip travel and living expenses, which can cost as much as $1,000 to $1,500 for a single weekend with two shows.

Judges must also deal with the mishaps of travel, like the rest of us. At one show, I saw a female judge in an unusual pair of flannel pants standing in the ring. I was musing about the odd color and pattern to a woman sitting next to me in the stands, who happened to know the reason for the interesting ring wear: the judge's baggage had been lost by the airline, and she'd been forced to get creative with her wardrobe. The pants were the bottoms to some pajamas she'd tucked into her carry-on bag! (Judge Chris Walkowicz has written a book on some of her experiences like this, well worth reading: *Dog Show Judging—The Good, the Bad, and the Ugly.*)

Judges must have proven and extensive knowledge of what is termed their primary breed (having bred and shown that breed). As they gain experience and move past the provisional stage of their careers, judges can apply to judge other breeds, and for that approval the requirements are not quite as exacting. Obviously judges are going to be more familiar with some breeds than others, it's impossible to be a true expert on every breed recognized by the AKC. People who know all about Boxers aren't necessarily going to be great judges of a toy dog like the Chinese Crested, for example. Most judges are responsible people who do their utmost to improve their understanding of new breeds by visiting well-known breeders, studying standards, and attending breed seminars. But the reality is that it can take many years of study and practice to truly understand a breed and its type. And the judges who aren't breeders have to rely on mentors to help develop their understanding of breed type—mentors who have their own preferences and prejudices. Judges may have good understanding of structure and movement and they can bone up on a breed standard before going into a ring, but if they haven't specialized in that breed, they aren't necessarily going to be the best judge of it. If they're really Hound experts, for example, they may prefer a gait in a Great Dane that is fast but not reaching enough.

It's especially hard to take when a judge puts up a dog for what seem like unfair reasons. One judge at a Texas show was heard to ask the steward which dogs in the ring were from Texas—a clear violation of rules. There are more subtle ways in which judges are affected, though, that are perfectly legal.

For example, the handler of the Best of Breed-winning dog will frequently mail the judge a copy of the win photo, which shows the dog, the handler, and the judge, with a note of thanks for the win. Very nice—and a great way to get the judge to remember you. (I've done this myself.) Sometimes owners or handlers will send the judge small gifts as well, though this crosses into a gray area of acceptability. But who's to know? The home addresses of the judges are listed in the judging program, and you could send anything you want with no one the wiser. I should emphasize that

I've never heard of a judge who took a monetary bribe. Of course, the good judges refuse blandishments like these and try to remain fair at each show.

How can they avoid the affects of advertising, though? There are dog magazines like *Dog News* and *The Canine Chronicle* delivered directly to every registered AKC judge that are filled with full-color ads with win pictures and announcing new titles, new points, new standings. There are breed-specific magazines handed out to judges at shows and specialty shows with the same ads, usually with text publicly thanking the judges that have awarded wins to the dog. And though the judge is not permitted to read the show catalog listing the names of the dogs in the show, their breeding, and their owners, it would be almost impossible for a knowledgeable judge not to recognize one of these top-winning dogs (usually with their famous handler on the other end of the lead) when they enter the ring. That must have a psychological effect. It's always safe to put up a top dog over others: no one will laugh at you and no one is likely to criticize your choice.

There are checks and balances on this unbridled discretion, however. Judges are critiqued and evaluated not only by handlers but by the AKC as well. As "provisional" judges of a breed, before becoming fully licensed, they must judge that breed in three different shows with an AKC representative watching and evaluating. After becoming a fully qualified judge, the AKC can still review decisions and results from any given ring, especially if there is a complaint made to the AKC representative at the show.

Even for a certified judge, there are plenty of unofficial evaluators. When a judge selects a dog as Best of Breed, that dog is then shown in Groups. A mediocre dog in the Group ring might be the result of a limited entry, or it might be something that causes other judges to question the ability of the judge that picked it. There's a special roped-off area for judges to sit ringside during Group judging, and they often sit and whisper among themselves as they look over the dogs coming into the ring and watch the ring judge make her choices.

The handlers are making their own assessments, too, and they can be quite vocal about complaining of unfair treatment from judges or about what they view as misconduct. All those eyes, and they're all assessing what they think about the merits of the dogs. It takes a brave judge to make an unconventional choice for Best of Breed, knowing that dog will be under the scrutiny of everyone standing ringside.

The people entering their dogs also "critique" a judge when they choose whether or not to show to her. If a judge has a reputation as political, choosing only pros and never owner/handlers, or if they simply don't seem to understand the standard, then word gets around. In the long run, people will stop entering their dogs to show under that judge. A small entry hurts the club sponsoring the show; they're counting on lots of dogs coming in order to cover the staggering costs of putting on a show. If a judge gets an unusually low number of dogs entered, and it happens repeatedly, word gets around, and that judge's assignments will begin to dry up and disappear.

Issues of biases, competency, and politics in the world of dog showing are all real. Advertisements, personal connections, and ingrained prejudices all exist as an unalterable part of the culture. This is no different, really, than any other field of human action, whether in the corporate world, the religious world or the social world. There are bad individuals in the dog show world, just as there is everywhere else. The key for me has been to stay as honest as possible myself, to learn who the trouble-makers are and avoid them, and to take as much joy as possible in just showing up with my spiffed-up gorgeous blue boy and trotting proudly with him into the ring.

CHAPTER 6
Yikes! The Money

Just owning a dog is expensive. When I bought Kunga I was amazed by his purchase price. I'd hunted around for Danes and seen comparable prices from almost every breeder in the country, but it certainly gave me pause to think of spending over a thousand dollars for what I thought was just going to be a pet.

But the purchase price of your dog is just the entry fee. After you bring him home, you have the enormous cost of vet bills (including vaccinations), food, treats, paraphernalia like crates and beds, and training. I buy dog food at a specialty retailer since it's premium stuff, costing $50 for a 30-pound bag. I go through a bag about once every two weeks. My friends Robert and Jen have a little rescued Yorkshire Terrier who eats about a cup of food a day. (They do spend more on little coats and hairpins for her, however.) I buy training treats, though fewer than when my dog was a puppy. The well-known Dane web site run by Linda Arndt (www.greatdanelady.com) suggests that a new owner should budget about $800-$1,000 in costs beyond the purchase price just to get a Dane puppy in the front door.

A study completed by the American Kennel Club in July 2004 estimated that the average one-time costs of a dog of any breed is about $2,100 (purchase price, supplies, and vet fees), and that average annual recurring costs are about $2,500 (food, regular vet care, toys, treats, etc.). Obviously, the annual costs decrease with the size of the dog (smaller dogs eat less, for one thing), which is probably why over a third of the respondents in that survey owned either a toy or small dog, whereas less than 7% owned a giant dog, like a Dane.

Lovable, but not cheap.

Just buying and owning a dog can be expensive; showing him will cost a whole lot more. In fact the decision to show a dog is another step into financial extremity. When I first proposed taking Kunga to a show, my husband asked, "How much money can he win?" When I told the members of the Great Dane club this story, it drew a guffaw because, of course, the answer is "a 39 cent ribbon." Showing is all done for the glory of the thing, I had to tell my husband. There's no monetary reward for showing a dog until you are in the stratosphere of showing, where a win can bring in thousands of dollars in prize money, and even that wouldn't cover the costs of getting there. Though some who show can make money from stud fees or puppy sales with winning dogs farther down the road, breeding is an expensive proposition (see Chapter 7), and will rarely return enough to repay the amount spent on showing. This is something to think through carefully before you get into the show world.

Showing your dog incurs a level of expense that can be breathtaking. There are entry fees, usually about $25-$30 per class for each show. Entry fees have been sailing steadily upward: when I first started showing Kunga in 2009, I generally paid $20-25 per class, but now the standard is $28 per class and is even $30 in some shows. To enter your dog in one class at the 2011 Great Dane Nationals was $35. It's even more for something like the AKC/Eukanuba show, which charged $50 per class in 2009, or Westminster, which was $75 in 2011.

If you want a guaranteed place to put your crate at the show, it generally costs another $25-$50 for reserved grooming space. I bathe Kunga myself at the dog wash for $15, and I save $10 by trimming his nails myself. (I used to pay a groomer to do his nails while I held him and tried to convince him that the nice lady with the trimming shears was not actually an axe murderer.) I cut off his whiskers—I've been assured this doesn't hurt him—with a relatively inexpensive pair of grooming scissors that cost me about $60 which would get me laughed out of the grooming area if I ever used these cheapies in public. I did try to use ordinary scissors, only to discover how big they seem when they're near Kunga's eyes and how tough those little whiskers are to cut.

Then there are the travel expenses to the show. I started with a Toyota Corolla with a well-used back seat, which Kunga fit into neatly. He snuggled into the fleece bedding that we won, fortunately, in a sweepstakes class (they're otherwise about $45) and which rested on top of the cordura seat cover ($120 plus shipping). I wrestled his crate onto the roof rack I had mounted on the top of the Corolla ($225 installed), because the crate didn't fit into the back seat with the dog, nor in the trunk.

I usually travel no more than about 7-10 hours at most away from home, and that far only rarely. If the show is close to home, I can drive there and back on show days and skip the cost of the overnight hotel stay, though the gas expense is higher for a multi day show. If the show is farther away, then we stay overnight and Kunga has to sleep in the room with me, for which motels seem to charge around $10-$30 extra per night as a "pet fee," even if there's no damage to the room. Though the spikes in gas prices can make the travel startlingly expensive, I still think I'm getting away so far with a pretty cheap travel budget, even though gas and lodging alone probably averaging $200 per show.

At one show I opened the back door of my car to allow Kunga to unfold himself from the back seat of the Corolla. Next to me, a man stood at the driver's door of a commercial-sized van and gaped. "Did that dog just come out of THERE?" he asked. Then he turned and pulled open the double doors of his giant vehicle, opened a crate inside, and attached a lead was a single Pug, all of about 10 inches high. His little girl waddled over to sniff noses with Kunga and it was my turn to be amazed. He brought that little animal in that great big van?!? Now we own a Honda mini-van in part so I can tow my dog around to shows in comfort and style.

As with everything else in dog show world, it's easy to go overboard with transport without even noticing that you've been leaning out of the boat of what the rest of the world considers normal. Big time show handlers have RVs they use to travel the country, and they need them. Most of the furniture in them is removed and replaced with crates of various sizes. Many show grounds have RV hook ups so they can access water and electricity and don't have to pay hotel fees. But I know plenty of people who are not professional handlers that have gone this route even though they have only one or two dogs. These RVs, you realize, get about 6-7 mpg and cost the earth to buy, even used.

Packing for a show, with crate cart, awning, pads, towel, show suit and shoes, food, pail, water, dish, folding chair, and grooming bag.

Once a dog has finished a championship of 15 points, he can go on to compete as a "special" indefinitely. People who show their dogs at this level expect to compete beyond the breed classes. They aim for the Group competition, and perhaps beyond that to the Best in Show class. As the dog wins, he accumulates points, and those points go toward determining things like the Top Twenty of each breed of dog in the country, or titles like top Sporting Dog or top Herding Dog. People showing their dogs with the intention of attaining these positions are said to be "campaigning" their dogs. Why do the points matter? Partly because Westminster, one of the most prestigious shows in the country, now only invites the five top dogs of each breed and getting such an invitation is a real honor for an owner. You can enter your dog for the remaining slots, but the competition is limited to champions only. The AKC/Eukanuba show invites only a limited number of dogs of each breed to compete. And people also care because the owners of the dogs have enhanced breeding prospects for their dogs and bitches—breeding can sometimes bring in high stud fees or high sale prices on puppies. Yet reputable breeders rarely make back their show and ownership costs with these fees. Prestige is what matters, not money. Dog showing, together with horse showing, may be one of the few pursuits in which esteem matters and the prize money doesn't.

What about those big-winning dogs that take home purses of $5,000 or more in the Eukanuba/AKC Nationals (or the smaller prizes in the two or three other shows per year that offer them)? A win like that doesn't defray a tenth of the cost of campaigning your dog for standings. To amass the number of points to be in the Top Twenty nationally, the dog must be shown nearly every weekend of the year, in the biggest shows available, and this game is only for those with big cash to pay the expense of it.

A specials dog almost certainly has a professional handler who charges anywhere from $50-$85 per class if you hand over your dog to her at the gate to the ring already cleaned, groomed, and trained—even more if the handler has to take on those chores. Handlers will generally be paid an additional fee if the dog wins his class and goes on to the Winner's Dog class, and again for going into the Best of Breed class, and yet again to take your winner into the Group class and (you wish!) the Best in Show class.

Owners at the higher levels of showing often choose to leave their dogs with the pros for both boarding and training the dog, as well as showing. These costs vary a great deal depending on how well known and successful the handler is, what region of the country you're in (the coasts cost more), and what kind of grooming and training the dog will require. It's much cheaper to send an experienced, shorthaired Chihuahua to a handler than it is to send a puppy Afghan hound, which eats more, requires more grooming and exercise, and must be trained for the show ring. The boarding charges start at about $5 per day for a toy dog and go up from there. A Great Dane handler will probably charge $15 per day, though generally handlers work out board on a monthly basis at a discount. Do the math: for 50 weeks a year, that's a minimum of over $1,700 just for basic living expenses. The handler may also take a retaining fee to ensure that your dog will get priority over other prospective owners who use the same handler. And if you win, there are show photographers who charge you to take "win photos."

And then there are all the travel expenses. Travel costs vary depending how much high living you do on the road. Most amateur owner/handlers like me stay in cheap motels and eat at the drive-through window at fast food places. Professional handlers often have an RV or motor home for traveling to shows, which has the added advantage of a kitchen to prepare their own food. The food at the shows themselves is usually deadly, and I mean that literally: high cholesterol, fatty, and chemical-filled. If you don't care for hot dogs or chips with cheap orange cheese spread, you may be out of luck. The primary benefit of show food is that it's fast, it's cheap (usually, unless you are in Madison Square Garden), and it's there on the show grounds. I find myself eating a lot of energy bars instead.

There are other expenses I could never have anticipated. For example, outdoor shows are often in city parks and held in areas with little or no shade. This necessitates buying some kind of awning, unless you want to scorch both you and your dog. The pop-ups come in various types, but the cheapest is about $120. I bought one to take to a show in Las Vegas and it worked well until the last day, when a windstorm whipped it sideways, tearing the fabric and twisting the metal until I had a very expensive piece of trash that I left in a can at the show grounds.

Advertising is an important part of campaigning your champion dog into the heights of breed placement. When show people talk about the influence of money in the show world, this is what they mean. Numerous dog magazines carry literally hundreds of advertisements, placed by owners in the hopes that judges will see and remember their dogs when they come into the ring. To advertise in the larger, all-breed magazines like *Dog News* or *The Canine Chronicle*, you're looking at prices of about $450 for a full-page color ad to $5,000 for the cover (which is an ad!). The breed-specific magazines are a bit less: a featured, color ad in the on-line *Dane World* now goes for $250; the front cover of the archive hard copy version is $900. The *Great Dane Gazette* charges the same for a full color ad and $1,100 for the front cover. Some people even advertise pups that haven't yet begun to show, and the costs continue as long as you show your dog. Most owners who want their dogs in the top rankings are advertising every month or every other month in their breed magazines, a Group magazine like *Working/Herding Dog* magazine, and in the all-breed monthlies. Apart from the magazine charge, these ads have to have photos (done by professionals, at costs that range from $125-$150 per session) and have to be put together by a graphic artist (an additional cost that can run to several hundred dollars per ad).

On top of equipment, handling costs, advertising, and handling fees, there are the supplies. Every show always has several vendors that set up booths near the rings from which you can purchase a wide variety of dog related items. Also, there are plenty of web sites and catalogs to peruse for the latest and greatest products. Show dog owners buy our fair share of the ordinary, dog-besotted owner merchandise such as little bandannas and bows, dog coats, comfy beds, and special vitamin supplements. But there's an array of show supplies that go beyond this. We buy grooming supplies like grooming jackets for ourselves (to fit over show clothes and keep the drool and hair off before the classes—from about $20-$45), specialty scissors (which can cost upwards of $150), and fancy shampoos with ingredients like rose, ylang-ylang, and shea butter (about $27 per gallon). And who with a long-coated dog can resist a rainbow-toothed specialty comb to carry into the ring (around $8)? There are heated kennel pads for cold grooming areas ($40-$120), and crate fans and cooling waterbeds ($120) for those hot summer outdoor shows.

My favorite crazy dog show item is a set of nail caps to slide over your dog's toenails to keep them from scratching and damaging that gorgeous, full show coat (about $70). Plenty of people can't keep their dogs in condition by running with them, or can't allow their intact, dominant male out in the dog park, so for them there's the doggie treadmill, starting around $400 for a small size. (Honest!)

The New York Times estimated in 2010 that it can cost upwards of $300,000 per year to show your special into the top tiers of dogs. The owners of a breed winner at Westminster in 2009 bragged that they'd spent a half million dollars campaigning their dog in that year alone. That included the cost of flying the dog around in their private jet to shows all over the country! Since reputations take time to build, even at 100 shows per year, a campaign to get a dog to be a serious prospect at one of the top shows (the National, the AKC/ Eukanuba National, and Westminster, sometimes called the "Triple Crown of dog shows") can last 2-3 years and cost nearly three-quarters of a million dollars.

Finding the money to show a dog can be tricky. Most top dogs are either owned by someone with pots of the stuff or have a patron—a co-owner who pays the bills. I've heard of people mortgaging their homes in order to show their dogs, but I hope that's a rarity. There are a surprising number of well-to-do business people who are working hard to support their dog show habit. One owner was telling me how much time and money she and her husband spent on their show dogs, and I asked her why she did it.

"What else are we going to do, play golf?" she asked.

An odd trend I've discovered is the attempt of one dog-loving spouse to hide the true costs of buying, raising, and showing dogs from the other. Dog show friends have joked and even bragged to me about the ingenious methods they've developed to keep expenses from their mate. This is far more frequent among women than men, but that may just be because there are many more women involved with dogs and showing than men. (The same seems to be true in the horse world.) Some of these ruses are simple, like saving pocket money by skipping the lattes or secretly car-pooling and saving gas money to spend on shows. One woman told me she'd even conspired with her accountant to shield her husband from full knowledge of what she was spending.

I began to wonder: who is making money out of this giant venture of dog showing? The numerous vendors of doggie merchandise from the practical (show collars and leads) to the extreme (tiny fleece dog coats sell well for toy dogs at the winter events) are probably making some money, or they wouldn't be at the shows. Many of the accessories you need for the show ring are more likely to be available from vendors at shows than from a local pet store. There are t-shirt booths, and places to buy food, and the ever-popular jewelry stores. Some of these vendors also sell their wares on-line. Virginia Perry Gardiner used to sculpt G.I. Joe action figures for a living. When I met her at her booth at Westminster in 2011, she sat behind tables filled with the exquisite dog jewelry she had made, with assistants helping the crowd of buyers choose their favorites. The display cases were filled with examples of nearly every breed of dog fashioned into necklaces, rings, earrings, and brooches. Ms Gardiner makes a good living out of this!

Others have figured out a way to make a living around the edges of the show world as well. My friend Debbie Towndrow, for example, got involved in the show world while she still had a day job. She acquired a Bernese Mountain Dog, a large, sturdy girl she named Brook. The puppy developed into a lovely bitch, and Deb turned her over to a professional handler. Deb watched from the sidelines, enjoying the shows, the dogs, and the people. And one day, she decided she would become a canine massage therapist. Soon she was very busy with her own practice, working out of an office during the week and traveling to shows on the weekends.

The immense amounts of money spent on advertising means that most breeds and even groups have their own dedicated breed magazines. One of them was started by Rita Suddharth. Rita began showing with a Great Dane, and was quickly pulled into the show world. Soon most of her friends were dog show people, and she was spending nearly every weekend at shows. In 1993, when the then-prominent breed magazine experienced trouble, Rita and a partner decided to start *Dane World.* Despite a full-time job elsewhere, Rita still publishes *Dane World* (online now, rather than in print) for the love of the breed and the dogs. You can find it at www.daneworld.com.

The show superintendent makes money, since they take a cut of the entry fees to set up the shows and run them.

The professional handlers are making some money, though many show only on the side and have day jobs. Even those who show full time vary widely in their annual income. Many make only about $45-60,000 per year gross—hardly a fortune. And while there are people making a good living as handlers, none are getting really rich. Many have other business ventures. Michael Brantley does very well as a professional handler, but also runs a boarding kennel with his wife as a sideline and as a project to support his handling work. (This is a pretty common means of supplementing handling incomes.)

Most judges don't make much from their work at the shows. Judges' fees vary depending on their expertise and how well regarded they are; the best get $800 per day, plus their travel and lodging expenses. Those are long days, however, beginning before the usual 8:00 AM start of the show and lasting for 8-10 hours of the show itself, most of that time spent on their feet in the ring. Many judges have day jobs, or are retired, or have spouses who support them. Some have jobs within the dog industry, giving seminars and workshops, writing books, or doing television commentary for big national shows. Some will spend more in travel, training, and continuing education than they make over their careers as judges. Like everyone else, the judges seem to be in it for the love of the dogs, and for the admiration and respect of their peers.

The show world is about prestige rather than the big bucks, even for breeders. They're the ones who are most interested in having champion dogs in their kennels, who want to advertise that their litters are bred from winners. But it's hard for me to see how any reasonably responsible breeder can make more than a nominal amount of money breeding dogs. The expenses of breeding often outweigh the return on the sale of puppies. No one I've ever heard of makes an actual living out of breeding, though many breeders have kennels that offer other services like day care, grooming, and training to pay the bills.

So on the whole, money drives the show world without actually being the motivating factor behind the showing. In fact, the show world has demonstrated some charitable inclinations. For example, one enlightened new organization that has appeared is "Take the Lead," organized in 1993 primarily in response to the surprising number of dog show professionals who were afflicted with AIDS. Several well-known judges, breeders, kennel club bigwigs, and other pros began raising funds to help people in the business pay their medical bills, insurance premiums, and even funeral costs. The organization started with a benefit cocktail party at a large regional show, during which everyone who attended received small lapel pins with the Take the Lead logo. These became a hot item over the next years, and soon the membership grew across the country. Go to any dog show now and you'll see nearly every professional handler with an up-to-date pin on her jacket or blouse, usually on the left side facing the judge! Take the Lead pays bills for showing professionals who need help with medicine, rent, utilities, transport to doctors or hospitals, and related services. From

1993 through 2010, the organization distributed nearly $3 million. They continue to host events and receive donations from breed clubs and individuals.

The Westminster Kennel Club supports a number of charities—from Take the Lead to the Guide Dogs for the Blind—and offers scholarships for veterinary students. Not many other kennel clubs have the funds to support charities, but some give gifts to local breed rescues and shelters. Our breed club, the Great Dane Club of Greater Denver, has given money to Great Dane rescue.

So though the show world is a costly place to be, it's not a place to make a lot of money. And it seems that show people can be as charitable as anyone else when the need arises.

CHAPTER 7
Breeding

From the time of the formation of kennel clubs, the most important element of dog shows has been the development of breeding stock. Though owner egos and prestige are at stake, the stated purpose of the conformation class is to pick the dog that most closely resembles the ideal for that breed. Get picked often enough, and the dog becomes a champion, and thus more desirable for breeding. If you get involved in the show world, you're going to learn something about breeding: some of it is funny and some of it is heart wrenching, but underneath it all it's supposed to be about trying to improve the breed.

When Kunga was about a year old, the time came to collect his semen so he could join the breeding dance. I talked to my vet, who referred me to a specialty reproductive practice located in a town about an hour away. Maybe I shouldn't have been so surprised that there should be specialists devoted to reproductive issues of dogs who run a facility to collect, analyze, and freeze semen for artificial insemination. Just as with cows, it's no longer necessary for the boy to meet the girl for puppies to appear. Breeders are no longer limited in their choice of studs by how far they're willing to travel; they can import fresh chilled or frozen semen from across the country, or even—as in Kunga's case—from across the world.

It never occurred to me to think through the process of semen collection, so I called the vet's office in advance to ask about it. Somehow I envisioned tubes and shots being involved.

"Do you have to sedate Kunga?" I asked the veterinary technician.

"Uh, no," she replied. "We'll just deal with him standing. We'll bring the bitch to him in a room."

"Oh, a bitch," I said. "Which bitch?"

"We'll call you when one of the bitches from the practice is in season, and you can bring Kunga in then."

"I see," I said, though I didn't. "And then what do you do?"

"Well, um, pretty much what you might expect," she said, not wanting to spell it out.

I suddenly realized what she was talking about. "You're going to masturbate my dog?!" I exclaimed.

In fact, that's exactly what happens. The vet asks that a client whose bitch is in heat allow him to use the girl as a teaser. The male is brought in to smell the bitch, and everyone hopes that nature takes its course. Of course the salient fact is that the dog doesn't actually mount the bitch; he is aroused enough for the penis to emerge, and the vet masturbates him until he ejaculates. The vet catches the ejaculate in a plastic condom, divides it into glass straws, then flash freezes it. A small amount is defrosted and examined under a microscope to be sure that the dog has mature and motile sperm and that there will be enough in the semen for at least a few breedings. If all's well, the vet determines how dense the sperm are, and therefore how many straws will be needed for a breeding.

With some trepidation, I put Kunga's sturdiest pinch collar on him and drove up to the vet's office one afternoon. A very kind owner of a Newfoundland bitch had agreed to allow her girl to be used as a teaser. She entered a small exam room and I brought Kunga in from the waiting room. Before they could even get the door closed, Kunga's penis was fully out of his sheath and he was nearly jumping with excitement. My eyes popped. Kunga was HUGE, and the penis had two bulges at the end of it. These, it turns out, are called the "bulb," and serve to ensure that semen doesn't escape during actual live mating.

"Whoa, big guy," the vet exclaimed, as he donned his plastic glove and readied the collecting condom. A few quick moments and it was all over, leaving Kunga happy but a little bewildered, and me relieved that I'd managed to keep him from actually getting on the bitch. It took much longer for Kunga to settle down and for his penis to retract into the sheath, a necessity for his health; the vets won't let you leave until that process is complete.

Once Kunga was in the breeding game, I got more interested in the business. When I had first started looking for a well-bred Dane, I was shocked at the purchase prices. Responsible breeders were charging $1,500 to $2,000 for a puppy. That included the first shots, papers, a health guarantee, and a requirement that if you ever wanted to get rid of the pup you had to return it to them. Even backyard breeders who provide no guarantees and are just in it for the money can charge $600-$800 for a puppy. It was certainly more than I'd expected to pay.

One of Kunga's puppies before his ears were cropped.

Since then, my breeder friends have educated me about the economics of bringing puppies into the world, and I can tell you it's not a money-making proposition for most of them. A breeder generally has the bitch only and has to find a dog whose traits will complement hers in order to produce puppies that—if the breeder is both wise and lucky—will improve on both the parents. This takes hours of research time, even for breeders who know the dog world well. Pedigrees going back 4-5 generations must be examined, photos studied, friends consulted. Many dogs carry genes for colors other than the coat they have, and that must be taken into consideration. Since there are no perfect dogs, the breeder has to assess both the strong and weak qualities of the bitch and dog, and try to discover whether either has the propensity for passing along those traits, for better or worse. For example, white markings seem to multiply in both blue and black Danes, and while they're acceptable if they're in the right place (chest or toes), they're considered less desirable. Height seems to get passed along easily, but substance—the strong bone structure—is harder to breed into puppies.

There are no guarantees with any breeding, so even after agonizing and planning and hoping, the breeder may not get what they hope for. It's a crapshoot, and an expensive one.

Before a bitch is bred to any dog, both should be health tested. This is true for every breed as a means to eliminate genetically transmitted weaknesses. (Unfortunately, not all breeds have adopted this philosophy. For some breeds there is very little health testing done even though it could demonstrably improve the health of the breed.) Beware and be informed about the standards for your breed. Breeding Danes should have tests on their eyes (the Canine Eye Research Foundation, or CERF, has a standard test and registers results), their hearts and thyroids, and an X-ray of hips and elbows, which allows a rating according to standards of the Orthopedic Foundation for Animals (OFA) or by PennHIP. Some of these tests are available at big shows, and this reduces the cost a bit. But generally all this testing will run at least $600 per animal. The same kinds of tests are run on other breeds, and they can help to clear genetically based diseases and weaknesses from those breeds as well.

Once the breeder has found what she hopes will be a great match, she has to get the owner of the dog to agree to the breeding. Generally this is not a problem if the bitch has been properly health tested and the breeder seems responsible. Figuring out just who is "responsible" isn't always easy. Just because a breeder has shown a dog doesn't necessarily qualify her as a good breeder, though it sure increases credibility when the dog or bitch has at least a few points toward a championship. Having the full set of health checks done helps to define a breeder as someone trying to assure the betterment of the breed. The purebred dog world is pretty contemptuous about what they call backyard breeders, and in most cases, rightly so. People breeding dogs without considering potential structural or other health problems are likely to produce unsound and unhealthy dogs. The innocent and ignorant buyers of these dogs end up with dogs with constant vet bills. The way breeders seem to distinguish between backyard breeders and the "responsible" ones is (1) to see if health tests have been done, (2) determine if the breeding dog has been shown in conformation classes or in other events like field trials, obedience, or agility, and (3) reputation within the breed. You can check the first two things by talking to the breeder. For reputation information, visit your local breed club, go to shows, ask friends in the breed.

I discovered that "AKC registration" means virtually nothing about the health or potential of a puppy. Any progeny of registered dogs can themselves be registered, and dilution of AKC registration has been so widespread that registration alone has come to mean precisely zero in the show dog world. Of course your dog has to be fully registered ("limited" registration means that offspring cannot be AKC registered) to show, but registration alone doesn't indicate a thing about its quality—so buyer beware those ads in the paper that trumpet: AKC papers! That's only a minimum requirement, not the be-all and end-all.

Once everyone has agreed to the breeding, there's a stud fee to pay. This can vary greatly depending on the quality, titles, and fame of the dog, anywhere from five hundred to several thousand dollars. Sometimes the owner of the dog will take first pick of the litter; that means one less puppy to sell, so it's still lost income even if it's not an up-front cost.

A "live cover," where the bitch goes to the dog and mates the old fashioned way, can be expensive if the dog lives a long distance away, since the bitch owner will incur all the travel fees. If the breeding is by artificial insemination, there are a lot of additional fees: collection of the semen, and testing to be sure it's motile (about $75-$100); shipping costs for the semen, including buffers and a shipping kit as well as Federal Express costs (about $100 for the buffer and kit, actual shipping costs depend on where the package is sent); progesterone testing for the bitch, to be sure that the insemination is done at the exact right time in her cycle (about $60-$75 per test, and performed anywhere from 2-5 times); and the fees for the vet to perform the actual insemination (ranging from about $75 for a simple vaginal insemination up to $700-$800 for a full anesthesia surgical insemination).

Once the actual breeding is done, there are tests to see if the bitch is pregnant, and more testing, such as ultrasound readings (from $75-$250 depending on location and vet), done throughout gestation. If the birth goes smoothly, all to the good. But there are numerous complications that can involve further vet bills, such as failure to deliver live pups, dead fetuses that must be removed from the dam, bleeding, and all the potential problems you can imagine with any birth. These can cost thousands of dollars when they involve surgery such as a C-section.

Generally a well-bred Dane will average 6-10 puppies, but they often have fewer, even single pups sometimes. Even if there is a full complement of puppies and all are healthy, there will still be some that are destined to be pets and some that are high enough quality to be shown, and sold to a "show home." Some breeders charge more for show dogs than pets, but many don't. After all, as my friend Loren points out, it costs the same per puppy to raise them, no matter how pretty they are. The breeder has to care for those pups for at least eight weeks before they go to their new homes, and this incurs costs for puppy formula, special puppy foods, and vet care and inoculations at a minimum. If there are any medical problems with the puppies, there are additional expenses.

If the breeder charges $1,500 per dog, they'll make $9,000 for a litter of six if they sell all of them and none are returned due to later circumstances of the new owners. Considering the costs outlined above, though, this could be about break-even!

Many breeders have homes for their puppies before they're even born: their waiting lists can be years long. Invariably, however, there are going to be puppies that don't quite cut it as show quality, and these puppies are sold as "pet quality" at lower prices to people who don't plan to show their dogs. There are often waiting lists even for these dogs, which are sold with a contract that requires the dog be spayed or neutered.

There are breeders out there who can't sell their puppies, no matter what they believe their quality to be. What happens then tells you something about the breeder. Friends of ours adopted a Labradoodle from one of the opportunistic breeders of these currently fashionable mixed-breed dogs. The puppy was slated to be euthanized because the breeder couldn't sell it. You will never find a responsible breeder who would do that unless something was seriously wrong with the health of the puppy. They will give any unsold puppies a home forever, if necessary.

When Kunga's semen was first collected, Cindy, the breeder from whom I purchased him, paid for the whole shebang (collection, testing, and storage). As its "owner," she gets to sell the semen however she chooses. Still, the first time she was asked to breed to Kunga, she called me to discuss it.

The request for Kunga's semen came from the owner of a fawn bitch. The woman raised blues, but had the problem common to many blue Danes in the U.S. of not having dogs that are "typey" enough. Many blues are too small in the head and too slight overall; some have coat problems where the true steel blue color browns or grays out. This breeder wanted to cross a fawn bitch who carried genes for blue with a blue dog, in the hope that at least some of the puppies would be blue, but have the substance of the fawn. In wanting to do so, she was planning to deliberately violate a taboo in the Dane world—the mixing of certain colors.

The stated policy of the Great Dane Club of America in its "Color Code of Ethics" is to prevent the mixing of colors in breeding Great Danes. Fawns and brindles may mate to each other, blacks and blues are acceptable partners, and harlequins can breed to mantles or blacks. But mixing these colors in other patterns is considered a violation of the color code even though the worst that comes from color mixing is strange colors or mis-markings—there are no adverse affects on the structure or health of the dogs associated with colors. (Some perfectly acceptable color crosses result in odd colors, too, and a harlequin-to-harlequin breeding can result in white dogs that are often deaf and/or blind.) If you want to raise the temperature of the room, ask a meeting of Dane people what they think of crossing the color lines. Feelings run high on both sides. This color discussion isn't limited to Danes, either—many other breeds have similar debates.

I never imagined this would be an issue for me. Kunga, of course, would happily mate with a Pekingese if she'd have him and he could work out the logistics. But when Cindy called about this proposed fawn breeding to Kunga, I had to do some research and think through what I had learned about the interbreeding of colors.

I found that the history of Danes is rife with cross-color matches. Harlequins, for example, once suffered from the same lack of type that blues do today. Decades ago, several breeders bred harlequins to fawns and brindles, trying to get a correctly colored harlequin who also had more of the size and type of the fawns. Today the harlequins have about the same range of size and substance as the other colors, partly as a result of this out-breeding to non-harlequin Danes in violation of the color code. For the same reason, look back into the pedigrees of champion blue puppies and very often you don't have to look back too many generations to find a fawn progenitor.

Technically, I didn't really have a say in Cindy's decision about breeding to the fawn. She paid for Kunga's semen collection and we had agreed that she would be the one in charge of deciding whether to approve a bitch when using this frozen cache. I imagine if I'd kicked up a big fuss, though, she wouldn't have agreed. As it was, I decided that I wasn't that upset about the idea. The owner of the bitch had tested her to be sure she carried for blue, she'd bred blue Danes for years, and she was aggressively trying to improve the blues, not just breeding for some exotic color she would then foist off on pet buyers. As it turned out, though, the fawn girl was, at six years old, too elderly to breed, and the artificial insemination didn't take.

This unorthodox breeding arrangement between a fawn and a blue, though it never produced puppies, arose because of the myriad ties between people in the show world. Like any community, from corporations in the same industry to medical associations, the connections run deep between friends and enemies who show dogs. When you head toward the show ring, you are rarely there without help, without owing people something. For example, Cindy sold me Kunga with "limited" registration because I didn't plan to show, then generously agreed to change the registration to be sure I could show him without charging me any additional fees. My friend Kathryn agreed to evaluate Kunga at that first Great Dane club meeting, and has been a source of encouragement and instruction ever since, and never charged me a dime. Carol taught me how to handle Kunga and continues to give me advice whenever I ask for it. Other club friends have come up to me after a show to give generous suggestions on how best to present Kunga or how to solve a problem we were having—and these people are my competition in the shows! Slowly the fabric of friendships and obligations is woven, and the newbie becomes part of the cloth of the show world.

This is a wonderful thing, but it is not without consequences. Cindy wouldn't ordinarily think about breeding a blue dog to a fawn bitch, but a friend of hers asked her as a favor to sell Kunga's semen to her.

A strand of the fabric was pulled again when my friend Carol approached me about using Kunga to breed to her black bitch, Ruby (Desertwood's LV Classy Hooker). This pairing is perfectly acceptable under the Color Code of Ethics, and had the added advantage that Ruby carried blue genes from her grandfather. The puppies would either all be blue, all be black, or there could be some with each color in the litter. The only complication was that Ruby was coming into season within a few weeks, and there was not enough time to complete all her health checks, something that was required of the bitch in Kunga's stud contract. As I'd agreed to do, I called Cindy to ask her whether this would be acceptable. (I always ask Cindy's advice about breeding, since I'm still very new to this and can use a more experienced view. Cindy doesn't charge for her help or share in the stud fee, she just helps out of friendship and a vested interest in seeing Kunga continue to produce good puppies, which reflects well on her breeding program.)

Cindy asked to see a photo of Ruby and to see her pedigree, and asked if I was friends with Carol. When I said yes, Cindy asked if Carol was a responsible breeder, and again I said yes. So, based on Carol's promise to complete Ruby's health checks after the breeding, we went ahead with Kunga's first live cover. This was something I wouldn't have done with anyone else, but it was a decision based on the friendships and connections built within the show world.

Ruby came into season at a dog show in Cheyenne, Wyoming. I'd left Kunga with Carol and Don to spend the next day with them in their trailer with a very interested Ruby. He slept in a crate near her and was obviously intrigued by the possibilities. They spent a day teasing each other before the ride home to Colorado.

By Monday, Kunga was wildly excited, and certainly in theory knew what was required for breeding. It was his execution that lacked effectiveness. We brought the two dogs together, and as soon as Ruby stood still enough for him to mount, Kunga placed his head over her back in preliminary courtship. This was accepted, so he tried to mount her. However he was facing perpendicular to her left side, and put his right paw over her back first. This meant that as he turned to mount, his rear was pointed at her face, a somewhat dangerous proposition when you consider the mouthful of teeth these dogs have. Swallowing my laughter, I pulled him off so he could try again. Once again, he came at Ruby from the side, and put up the wrong paw; but this time he put the other up beside the first, so that he was standing his weight right onto her back. Poor Ruby couldn't hold him like this for long, and she began to sink to the floor in a slow plié under Kunga's weight. Kunga was panting and jumping with excitement but didn't have a clue how to manage the deed. We pulled him off Ruby again, with me laughing so hard that I could barely keep hold of the leash.

Carol looked at me as I stumbled backward, helpless with laughter, and suggested tactfully that maybe I'd be more use holding Ruby. We switched positions and the next time Kunga mounted he managed to hop around to the proper position, though he needed Carol's help to actually complete the connection—no small feat with a 150 lb dog. I was bent double, trying to stifle my guffaws in the interest of not distracting either dog from the business at hand. All this was surprisingly difficult for the humans, and we were both sweaty and breathing hard. Carol, kneeling on the floor beside the dogs, was bruised from shoving Kunga into position and trying to keep out of the way of his dancing feet when she looked up and said, "Remind me again why we don't raise Chihuahuas?!"

Kunga eventually accomplished what's called the "tie," when the bulb of the penis is so far into the girl that neither dog can pull away from the other. This is important because it's during this tie that the insemination occurs. Kunga's first tie lasted a bit over twenty minutes, during which poor Ruby groaned several times in discomfort. Mating is painful for the bitch, and they'd never do it if their hormones didn't lure them into it. Finally the two gracefully stepped away from each other, and Ruby made it clear she didn't need Kunga's company in her house any longer. We put the two together again the following day, just to be sure.

Sixty-three days later, right on schedule, Ruby gave birth to eleven puppies, two of which were stillborn, and one of which died soon after birth. That still left eight puppies, some blue and some black, all round as baked potatoes and covered with wrinkles. Their eyes were closed and their little footpads were pink and new.

Everything went well until a week after birth. Very suddenly the puppies became sick and listless, and in one day four puppies died unexpectedly. These deaths were utterly mysterious, and a horrified Carol and Don rushed the remaining pups and their dam to the vet.

The diagnosis: fading puppy syndrome. This is not exactly an illness, but a collection of symptoms that point to an illness. Ruby apparently had contracted a virus during her pregnancy that didn't affect her at all, but damaged the puppies' immune systems. This is the most frequent cause of fading puppy syndrome. The pups seem fine at birth but—almost always in the first week—they begin to die of secondary infections as well as from the virus.

Carol organized a rotation of helpers who would take shifts giving the puppies antibiotic shots, shots of extra fluids, and feed them with eyedroppers filled with beef broth and Pedialite. I took my turn, feeding every pup or helping it to nurse every half hour. I sat there for hours on the floor of the whelping box, telling each puppy how great a life it could have if only it would live. I stroked Ruby's head to encourage her to stay still longer and let the pups nurse as much as possible.

Over the succeeding weeks, despite unceasing around-the-clock care, two more puppies died. It was devastating to watch. My happiness at seeing Kunga's first litter was made bittersweet by these deaths.

Since it was impossible to tell the long-term effects of the virus on breeding, the two remaining pups were neutered and sold as family pets, and I hear that they are living happy lives. Ruby was spayed and has been learning to compete in AKC rally events rather than continuing her conformation show career.

Though Kunga has since been bred successfully and has sired some lovely pups (some show quality, and I'm eager to hear how they do in the show ring), I've never forgotten the sadness that came with his first litter. For me, it was another lesson in the hazards of breeding. Not only is it unlikely to make you money, it can break your heart.

CHAPTER 8
Winning

Some people have little rituals they do before heading into the show ring to settle themselves or their dogs, or to nod to superstition with "good luck" gestures. My ritual begins with the show bath, when I lead Kunga into the tub at the grooming shop. When the bath is finished, he is transformed in my mind from my pet to a big gorgeous show dog who's going to WIN!

I love my dog even when he loses, and I don't love him more when he wins. But winning is a whole lot nicer. "Whoever said that it's not whether you win or lose that counts, probably lost," said Martina Navratilova. My husband asked me once whether I would show Kunga if I knew I had absolutely no chance whatsoever of winning, just for the enjoyment of doing something with my dog. Nope, I had to reply. It's not that much fun. If I never won with Kunga at all and it became clear he was not show quality, I would have stopped showing him. We are all in the ring because we want to win and think we can.

Winning is addictive, like gambling. The strange thing about winning at a dog show is that you're not responsible for the win, the dog is. Yet we get a rush when we win. We all run around pumping our fists in the air when it's a particularly great win, like a big major or those last points that finish the dog's championship. Scientists at the University of Cambridge in England have found that "near wins" help to keep gamblers coming back to the tables, because the brain is fooled into believing that it is learning something and might win next time, even though the person is playing a game of chance. I think the same thing happens with showing, so that when you get a reserve, or you've won before, the result lures you back to the ring to try again.

The result of a good weekend's showing! From left to right: blue ribbon for winning a class; purple ribbon for Winner's Dog; blue and white ribbon for Best of Winners; and the coveted purple and gold for Best of Breed.

Sometimes you win when you do not expect to, and while it is nice, it can lead to mixed feelings. At one show, for example, I had struggled to get Kunga to behave. He was acting like the teenager he was: wiggling and jumping and turning around to try to meet the dog standing behind us. He just wouldn't hold still during the stack and kept charging forward when we tried to move around the ring. He was nearly out of control, I was embarrassed and upset, and when I looked up after the last section of the class the judge pointed at me. "Take him around alone," the judge said. Now I felt truly awful and exposed as I pulled out of line and took Kunga around again. He behaved well then, but I was astonished when the judge pointed at me as we finished the circle and said, "Winner's Dog." Kunga had won despite his behavior.

Though I was pleased with the points, this made me feel a bit odd. Should I be glad of a win when I didn't think Kunga had shown well? I can tell you I didn't go to the superintendent's table and try to convince them to take away the points! It happens sometimes, and we resent it when it happens to other people's dogs—they win when we don't think they should.

When you show in a certain geographic area, you tend to see the same dogs over and over, and they're often owned by your friends in the local breed club. Going to a local show means seeing my Dane club friends with their dogs—both outside the ring and inside the ring—competing with Kunga. It can be strange to win over friends who are in the ring with you, even when you think you should. Some clubs are cauldrons of bitterness and ill will, but fortunately our local club is not: we are pretty civil and cheer for each other. No one has ever made me feel badly when Kunga won over their dogs, and I've tried to return the favor. After all, we are club members after the show is over. We just have an unspoken agreement that we all think our own dogs are the best!

Sometimes the winning dogs are extremely unlikely, and that can bring the most satisfaction of all. One of the happiest winners I ever met was the owner of a Saluki at the Texas Kennel Club show in 2009. I met her ringside as she waited to take her Saluki into the Hound Group for judging, having won Best of Breed earlier in the day. She was so relaxed and glad to have me pet her dog that I didn't realize she was about to show him until the steward called the class.

Her husband smiled as she proudly trotted into the ring with this lovely, long-limbed dog. I asked him about the dog's pedigree and was flabbergasted when he told me he'd never seen the dam or sire: the Saluki was a rescue dog! This is nearly unimaginable in the show world. When my jaw started working again, I asked him how that had happened. He told me that he and his wife raise Salukis and are active in the Saluki rescue club in their area. One day the club called to ask that they check into an owner who wanted to surrender her dog to a shelter. When they visited, they found a woman who hadn't a clue what a Saluki was like before she decided she wanted a purebred dog. Her lack of experience and unwillingness to learn anything about the breed meant that most breeders she found refused to sell her a puppy. She went on to the web and managed to convince a breeder in Eastern Europe to sell her a Saluki. Within months, the new owner was overwhelmed by the needs of this highly-strung dog. She didn't neuter him, couldn't housetrain him, and hadn't figured out how to feed him properly. The rescuers took him in on behalf of the rescue club and spent a few weeks feeding and training the dog. They began to suspect that he could be a very elegant specimen and called the previous owner to ask if she still had his AKC registration papers. She did, and agreed to sign the dog over. Now he is a champion, and that day as Saluki #11 he took fourth in the Hound Group.

Winning is really about the ego of the people, not the dog. Though there are dogs who love to show and light up when they get to prance around the ring, it's the people who care about the win itself. And the people can sometimes really go overboard in what they're willing to do in order to win. Winning has become so important to some people that they bring dogs to the ring that shouldn't be there for other reasons. In the rush to produce a beautiful dog, breeders sometimes ignore the character or temperament of the dogs they're producing.

Every breed has its own horror story of breeders who have beautiful dogs but are known to care less about the temperament these dogs have. One handler told me of going into the ring to handle a male Akita as a favor to the breeder, who was already in the ring with the male's littermate. When for some reason his sister screamed out—the breeder might have stepped on her foot—the male began to growl. The handler, an experienced Akita owner, reached down and firmly but gently took hold of his ruff. "That's enough," she said. Instantly, the male leapt up, snarling and flat-eyed, and went for the handler's throat, and she was suddenly in a struggle for her life. There was a shocked silence in the ring as both handlers and onlookers tried to take in what was happening. It would have been insanely dangerous to approach with another dog on the lead, so the handlers in the class were helpless. The judge shouted to get the dog out of the ring, but the handler couldn't; if she let go of the dog's ruff to catch hold of the leash she would have given him the chance to lunge at her throat. Finally, another handler who knew the dog ran into the ring, got behind the dog, and grabbed its collar and the back of its neck. Calling his name, she finally managed to get the attack stopped and the dog settled. It was, of course, disqualified for life from showing.

Judges can excuse a dog from the ring for "threatening or menacing" behavior, and they are supposed to record this reason for asking the dog to leave. There is a "three-strikes" rule, so that if your animal is violent in the ring three different times, it can be disqualified from showing permanently. If judges (or breeders) ignore aggression or fear or hesitation, those qualities may get bred into the next generation of dogs. Winning then becomes a way of perpetuating a lovely structure at the cost of the wrong kind of temperament.

Owners are willing to spend a lot of money in pursuit of winning, but some are also willing to spend quite a lot of time away from their dogs in order to have a champion. Many show dogs live with their handlers on the road a good part of the year, some for years on end, and rarely even see their owners as they campaign for points. I wonder what kinds of relationship owners have with those show dogs? Certainly a different one than I have with mine. One handler friend of mine has a lovely Bulldog bitch that he showed for several years. When the time came to retire the dog, its owners gave her to the handler. After all, "home" for that girl had come to mean wherever the handler was.

Over the years, my friends and mentors have taught me some lessons about what helps to make a winning show dog. Though of course the dog must start with the requisite good structure, there are certain personality traits and learned behaviors that help any dog to do better in the ring. I call these the "7 Habits of Highly Effective Show Dogs" (with apologies to Stephen Covey). Having them doesn't guarantee success, but they all contribute to winning.

The first of these habits, believe it or not, is eating. Even a dog that eats well at home can get picky on the road. Early in his show career I took Kunga to Topeka, Kansas for a five-day cluster of shows. It was mid-August and about a zillion degrees with humidity up near swamp level. From the first exposure to the sights and smells of that large show, with many bitches in season, Kunga stopped eating. For five days I tried everything, but he had only half a hamburger one day and a dish of vanilla ice cream another day. I learned that this is typical behavior for a male dog when exposed to bitches in heat.

People offered numerous remedies, all aimed at disguising the scent of the luscious canine ladies: Vaseline or vanilla extract or lavender oil on Kunga's nose or on his upper lips. But I couldn't bring myself to end what was probably Kunga's favorite aspect of showing, smelling the whole shebang.

Since that grueling experience, Kunga has reverted to type and now eats whatever I feed him, show or no show, at home or on the road. It means he doesn't lose energy or condition when we travel, and both of us show better for it.

The second habit is equally obvious: your dog must be able to sleep! And he has to do it anywhere and everywhere possible. The first time I left Kunga alone in a crate in a grooming area, he went nuts, crying and pawing at the door and worried about when I'd return. At that point, I still hadn't learned to put a big blanket across the crate, both for warmth and a little sense of privacy and security. It's mayhem in the grooming areas, with barking dogs, screaming dryers, clanging crates, and running people, all making it difficult for a dog to settle down and rest. But Kunga quickly caught on to the fact that I'm certainly coming back to get him, and now he just flops down and goes to sleep in the crate. The first time my friend Carol saw that, she approved mightily: it's hard to relax and a dog that can sleep at the show is one that has an advantage.

Another thing that took some time was getting Kunga to sleep in strange motel rooms. Our first road trips were up-all-night marathons, with him pacing around and barking at the sounds of the people in nearby rooms and dogs in the hallways. Once he decided we were not likely to be attacked, though, Kunga calmed down. He now sleeps well no matter where we are, as long as I'm there too.

Habit number three: the dog copes well with the chaos of changes in routine. Shows can involve a lot of changes to the dog's schedule, and dogs hate change. To make an early morning ring time at a show hours from my house, I have to get up especially early and get on the road. This can mean Kunga doesn't get his breakfast until much later in the morning than he's used to, or that his dinner is delayed until after we get home in the evening beyond his usual time. Driving for long periods can be hard on both of us. Kunga's sleeping becomes haphazard, and he never knows when he'll get the chance to pee and poop. All these deviations from normal can upset a dog terribly, and those who can't get used to it will learn to hate show days.

Number four on the list is that the dog actually likes people. There are hundreds, even thousands of people at shows, and not all of them know good dog etiquette. A stranger who wants to cuddle with an adorable toy dog can scare the bejesus out of the animal just before it goes into the ring and spoil its performance. Many children are not taught even basic manners around dogs and will run at them (or away from them, which can set off a prey drive in hunting dogs) screaming, reaching for the face and head. Shy dogs will be overwhelmed and can show poorly after being frightened or petted over-enthusiastically. Fortunately, most show dogs have learned to take all this in stride, and actually enjoy meeting new people. Kunga is utterly trustworthy with people, thankfully, and I never hesitate to allow even the loudest little kid to pet him.

The fifth habit is similar to the fourth: dogs have to be able to cope with other dogs. Obviously dog shows are filled with dogs, most not neutered or spayed, and many that will challenge one another in the grooming or exercise areas. Kunga likes little dogs but doesn't much like other large dogs, including Danes. Until he was about two, he mixed well with all the dogs that showed up ringside, sniffing and friendly. But once he reached his sexual maturity—and after his first live cover—he became much less friendly to other dogs. This is an ongoing difficulty ringside, and means that I usually wait some distance away while the other dogs take their turns. (Kunga has never been belligerent *inside* the ring, even standing flank to shoulder with a dozen other dogs and bitches crowding into a corner waiting their turns for examination.) But a dog that likes other dogs and is at ease around them will be a happier and more effective show dog.

Number six never fails to amuse my non-show friends: the dog poops and pees on command. This is a useful habit even for pet dogs, but show dogs that do it are at an advantage. A nervous dog that inhibits its usual bowel and bladder movements, because he's not sure where or when to go, is not going to be comfortable in the ring. Who could run in circles and stand up straight if they have to go to the bathroom pretty badly? Shows are busy places for the handlers, and there is not often a lot of time for "exercise"—so its best if the dog can learn to go when the time is available, on command. My grooming area was once next to that of a few Cavalier King Charles spaniels whose owners showed me their trick to deal with unwilling dogs. They stuck a match (unlit!) up the butt of their dogs, and quickly produced a bowel movement. Supposedly the phosphorous of the match head stimulates the dog to poop, though I've also heard that it's just the object itself that produces the effect. It's a trick I've seen used a lot.

Puppies especially are prone to going in the wrong place, and every steward's table has a roll of paper towels for cleanups when accidents happen in the class. The rule, by the way, is that the steward will hold your dog while you clean up after it. Often the stewards are nice enough to clean up the mess themselves; they're dog people, after all. Once, a Dane puppy decided to pee during his class during the down and back, leaving a gigantic puddle in one corner of the ring which far exceeded the ability of a few paper towels to dispose of. A cleanup crew with mop and bucket was called, but the judge decided to proceed while we were waiting for them. This made the movement portion of the examination pretty alarming as the exhibitors tried to cut off that corner when they ran around the ring.

Finally, the seventh habit is what I call charisma on command. There's something extra special about a winning dog that goes beyond temperament and bone structure, a show-off's quality that exhibits itself in the ring. The dogs that have it, or can learn to turn it on, have a distinct advantage. Sometimes it shows itself as a connection between the dog and judge. I can always tell within about a minute of being in the ring if Kunga has the chance of winning that day. There's some kind of energy that he can turn on, seemingly at will, which makes him lift his head, extend his neck and back, and pop his ears forward. It has nothing to do with what's going on outside the ring (though once a well-placed squirrel at an outdoor show did us a great favor by running up a tree near the ring), or with bait I'm holding. I think it may be a response to the interest of a judge, which you can feel like an electric charge in the air when it's directed at your dog. Judges vary a lot in how fair they are to each exhibitor; some will barely glance at your dog or do a perfunctory examination that doesn't include all the requisite parts. Others, even though they have given an equal amount of time to your dog, radiate their disinterest. But on those occasions when a judge actually likes Kunga and is considering him as a winner, I can feel it and I think Kunga feels it too. He always performs better when it happens. But a truly great show dog would be able to switch on this charisma whenever it's asked of him. Sometimes you'll hear a judge say she awarded a win because the dog "asked for it," which means that dog has thrown the switch and demanded the attention of everyone in the ring. I wish I knew where that button was on Kunga!

Michael Brantley likes to say you can choose what level you want to be at in this sport. You can find a dog, train him yourself, take him into the ring, and spend a year or two or three to gain him a championship. Or you can decide to make the sacrifices, both financial and emotional, to take your dog up a level. This entails more money, probably to hire a professional handler, and to enter more shows that are farther away from home. It probably also means advertising at least a little. With this kind of investment, you might get a dog with a championship, a grand championship (a new level of titles recently instituted by the AKC), and perhaps even move into the top twenty of your breed. Or you can go all out, hire handlers, send your dog away for months or years, advertise heavily, and perhaps—just maybe—have a top-ranked dog with a chance at Group and Best in Show wins at the big shows and at the "triple crown" shows of National, Eukanuba, and Westminster. There are income limits to playing with your dog at these higher levels, but if you have the cash, nothing stops you from trying. If you decide to show your dog, you have these choices to make, and all of them pit your ego against your relationship with your dog.

I went to the Westminster Kennel Club in 2011 to see some of the top-winning dogs in the country. These dogs compete at a different level than Kunga and I ever have, and the air is different in the stratosphere of these shows. Finishing your dog as a champion is only the first part of a show career for some of the best. Going on in competition as a special is another world altogether as the focus becomes competing in Groups and Best in Show. It is where the stakes are increased and where money and politics and gossip can combine into a bitter brew or an exciting elixir, depending on your taste. Some people thrive in this world, whereas others become scarred by it and retreat as soon as possible. It is significantly different to play in this arena, and substantially more expensive.

The competition at the Westminster Kennel Club show is emblematic of the world of the "special," the dogs who are at the tops of their breeds in points won through the previous year. Westminster KC puts on its annual all-breed show in February of every year, and it is one of the three biggest events on the show calendar. The show is often televised, sometimes live, and for people who know nothing about showing, it's probably the only event they can name involving dogs.

Everyone I talked to had the same reason for entering their dogs in this premier event: they think there's a chance, however remote, that on that day, their dogs will win. I sat next to an owner of a Bichon Frise—a little white dog with hair teased and pouffed into a cloud around its body—who had taken just as much time in grooming herself as the dog in the ring. She was one of the "pulled, painted, and frosted" crowd, well-to-do women who have spent a lot of money on their personal appearance with facial surgery, make-up, and "done" hair. I always thought these people were cynics, but this lady was as starry-eyed as a new mother when her little bitch walked into the ring. There was a huge entry, and there was plenty of time to talk with the owner as the dogs were paraded around the ring. She chattered away about her dog's breeding, the silly tricks it did at home, how absolutely adorable it was and superior to this or that other one in the ring with her. So, I asked, do you think your girl will win? The owner surprised me a bit when she answered no, of course not, and pointed to a handler in the ring with another dog.

"He'll win," she said.

"How do you know?" I asked.

"Oh, he's been handling it for a while, and there's a lot of money behind it," was her answer.

Sure enough, she was correct: that dog did win Best of Breed and went on to compete in the Non-Sporting group. In fact, during the two days of the show, most of the owners I sat next to were able, in advance, to point out the dog (or the top two likely dogs) that was going to win Best of Breed. Over and over, for Welsh Terriers, Danes, Bloodhounds, and nearly all the other breed rings I visited, the owners accurately predicted the outcome. Their reasoning was always the same: the money, the handler, and the judge's preferences for a certain quality such as movement over other qualities like angles of the body. One friend I visited after her dog lost to the predicted winner summed it up: it was her opinion that at this level of showing, only about 25% of the outcome is predicted by the quality of the dog. The rest, she said, is money spent, the fame of the handler, and the prejudices of the judges.

So why are the expected losers there at all, if they think the winners are almost a foregone conclusion? It seemed to me that everyone at Westminster was captured by the spell of the show, by the possibility of an upset, by the magical thinking that said, "Hey, I have a good dog, I've put my money on it, too, and I could walk away with that ribbon." If the usual suspects won in the ring, though, there were some valuable consolation prizes. There's the "Best of Opposite Sex" winner and up to three "Award of Merit" winners. These are recognitions of the quality of the dog without the actual win, and can mean a lot to owners and breeders.

Even though everyone at Westminster is there to win, there is another, even more prevalent, motivation for being at the show—the satisfaction of seeing their dog in one of those famous rings, with the green carpet and the gold sign posts holding up the purple and gold class lists. The setting is spectacularly high-class, and the Westminster people know how to put on a show. Just being in Madison Square Garden, with this august company, is enough for most owners.

I came back from my trip to Westminster a bit depressed about what it takes to win in our sport. I didn't have much time to dwell on it, though, since the next day I had to get Kunga ready to show at the Denver cluster of shows—five show days that bring hundreds of exhibitors and spectators to the National Western Stock show complex. This cluster was the same one where Kunga and I had shown for the very first time, and the competition hadn't gotten any easier since then. There were three and four point majors for each day of the schedule, and dogs came from all over the West to compete. We had over 40 Danes from Idaho, Colorado, Nevada, California, Texas, Oklahoma, Arizona, New Mexico, and Nebraska.

Kunga had 14 points by this time and only needed one point to "finish" his championship, but I wasn't holding my breath. There were a lot of gorgeous dogs competing in these shows.

To give you a sense of how subjective dog show judging can be, we had five different Best of Breed winners in five days, from the same pool of dogs entered. Don Volleberg handled a dog nicknamed Hunter to Winner's Dog twice, but the other three days three different dogs won, and Hunter didn't even win his class.

On Friday, I entered the ring with Kunga up on his toes with excitement, as usual. His tail wagged when the judge approached, he nudged onlookers outside the ring while we were waiting our turn to stack up for examination, and he's still very interested in meeting all those girl dogs, especially when they arrive at the show in heat. (It's permissible to show a bitch in heat, but it does tend to heighten the excitement of all the dogs around the ring. It can even be a handler's trick to bring a bitch in season to the ringside as early as possible to thoroughly distract the boys that she might compete against later.)

Kunga had that electric charisma that he seems to be able to turn on sometimes, prancing and full of himself. The judge smiled as she approached for the first time, and said, "He's such a happy dog." She chose him as class winner, and we re-entered the ring a few minutes later for the Winner's Dog class. It was a big class, with the winners of the puppy classes, Bred-by class, and the Open classes for Brindles and Fawns in addition to Kunga. Since she had already seen (and chosen) all these class winners, the judge didn't take too much time with us. We lined up and stacked our dogs while she took a good look at us all. Then she had us move around the ring together at a fast clip, each handler hustling to make her dog look great. "Hup, hup," I whispered to Kunga, patting him on his chest and taking off at the front of the line. Around we all went in a blur of coat colors and wagging tails, until we came back to the start position. Once again, everyone set up their dogs as quickly as possible for that last good impression. After looking over all the competition, the judge pointed to Kunga and said, "That's my Winner's Dog."

Kunga was finished!

As I crossed the ring to get the purple ribbon, I realized that nearly every other handler of the dogs who were competing with me in the ring for those points was cheering, and a few were pumping their fists and whistling for us. Outside the ring, too, there was a roar of approval from my friends and people from the club, all of whom realized that Kunga had just finished his championship, possibly the first natural-eared blue to do so in Colorado. You could hardly hear my thanks to the judge as I trotted Kunga up to her, and I wasn't even completely out of the ring as people began coming up to hug me and shake my hand. I was crying, and even a few of my friends had tears as they congratulated me on the end of a two-year odyssey to make Kunga a champion.

It was this that made the whole journey worthwhile. I felt the warmth of happiness in my chest, not for the win—I still didn't quite realize that Kunga was now a champion—but for the camaraderie and the support that my friends had shared with me. There they were, cheering for someone who had really just entered the show world, who knew nothing about it twenty months before.

Of course I called my husband first with the news. You could almost hear him smiling over the phone. As we were about to hang up, he asked, "Is Kunga happy?"

Once again, this wise man had made me take a step back and see this in perspective. Kunga was happy because I was happy. He didn't have a clue, of course, what a purple ribbon meant, but he bounded around at the end of the lead as people came up to congratulate me. I had very little to do with the winning: I had just learned not to be too inept as I stood Kunga up and moved him around the ring. And I only accomplished that through the kindness and generosity of my friends who gave me advice when I did things wrong and cheered me on when things went well. It was Kunga's looks and character, bred into him by Cindy and others along the tail of his pedigree, which had won him the fifteen points. And he didn't care at all. He did, however, enjoy the unexpected hamburger treat after the classes were finished. He's just a dog, after all.

Kunga's happiest when we're playing outside together. He doesn't care about winning at all.

APPENDIX
Finding a Good Breeder

THERE ARE LOTS OF NICE RESCUE DOGS. I've owned some myself. Breed rescues and humane societies all have plenty of pet dogs who need homes, and this can be a great way to go if you want a dog. You can Google "[name of breed], [name of your state]" and get some idea of the dogs available from local breed rescue groups. You can also go to the local animal shelter and find a wide assortment of dogs that need homes. I think rescue is needed and honorable work.

But when I wanted a Great Dane, I didn't turn to a local shelter, or to the Great Dane rescue in my state, because I just didn't think I could cope with a Dane that might have health or mental problems. Danes get BIG, and I'm reasonably small and not really interested in a major emotional struggle to get control of a sad or damaged dog. Danes, like a lot of other dogs, can get withdrawn and gentle with abuse or neglect, or they can get aggressive and sly. It takes patience and time to deal with either problem, and so far I just haven't felt I could do that with a dog that weighs at least half again what I do.

Health is frequently a big problem with rescued Danes. Early nutrition is critical; if fed an ordinary puppy diet, Danes get too much protein and can grow too fast for their bodies to develop coping mechanisms. If they aren't fed enough, they don't grow properly either, and can have weak joints that will be a nightmare further down the road. THERE ARE LOTS OF NICE RESCUE DOGS, but I didn't want to take the chance on a difficult one if it was going to be as gigantic as a Great Dane. If this is a moral failing on my part, not to be able to take on these kinds of unknowns, so be it. I wanted to get a dog that had the best possible start in life and take responsibility from there. I began to search for a breeder.

The hunt for a healthy dog can be challenging if you don't know how to tell the good breeders from the bad ones. Be particularly wary of the advertisements in the newspapers for puppies; they're from backyard breeders who almost certainly don't do health checks on either the sire or dam, who haven't thought through the breeding carefully, and who probably won't provide much in the way of information or support after you bring the puppy home. If you come across a breeder eager to sell you a dog without knowing who you are or whether you can deal with a dog, you're dealing with either a backyard breeder or a puppy mill.

There doesn't seem to be any easily accessible, centralized public database with information on puppy mills. States generally lack enforcement personnel to stop any but the most egregious breeders: those who are outright abusive and cruel to their dogs in an obvious way who are reported to the authorities. Quieter high-volume breeding operations churning out puppies for the holiday markets are rarely on the radar. All this means that the general public has almost no access to information on bad breeders of puppy mills, so these breeders continue to thrive. Buyer beware.

Another warning siren should go off if the breeder won't let you visit their premises or won't allow you to touch or hold the puppies (though very young puppies may be off limits for touching during the first couple of weeks of life). Any good breeder wants to show off their breeding stock and will be glad to have you visit. In fact, some breeders insist on meeting you face-to-face before they'll even discuss allowing you to take home one of their puppies.

In contrast to a backyard breeder or a puppy mill operator, a good, reputable breeder should tell you anything you want to know about the mama and papa, including their health, their previous offspring, their training, and even whether they prefer playing with balls or chew bones. A good breeder will want to know every detail of your life that's relevant to you having a dog. A good breeder will provide a guarantee that if you decide later that you don't want the dog, or if it has health problems, you can give it back at any time in its life. In fact, good breeders have dire clauses in their sales contracts that force you to return an unwanted dog to them rather than to a shelter or rescue organization. It just takes too long and too much work to build a reputation to have it ruined by some hopeless shmoe who can't deal with their dogs. I know one breeder who will even offer a free puppy from a later litter if the dog she sells you dies as a result of anesthesia while being neutered or spayed!

Good breeders do health checks. For Danes, this includes checks of the eyes, heart, thyroid, and hips for both male and female. Other breeds may have different problems and different standard health tests. Sadly, health checks are not standard in certain breeds. The standards for health checks in other countries is also different; in Australia and New Zealand, it's a rare breeder who does any health checks, and then probably only for hips. It's buyer beware for those searching abroad for a show puppy. Be sure to research your breeder and scrutinize the pedigrees very closely.

Go to the local or national breed club web site to find out what health testing is relevant to the breed you're looking for. Everyone keeps copies of these health certificates; ask to see them before buying a puppy. Any responsible breeder will be delighted that you know enough to ask and will be happy to show you proof that their dogs are healthy. You can also go to the Canine Health Information Center ("CHIC") at http://www.caninehealthinfo.org to see a record of health checks on purebred dogs. CHIC is a database organization jointly sponsored by the AKC Canine Health Foundation and the Orthopedic Foundation for Animals. They keep records for each dog of completed health checks. If your breeder can give you a "CHIC number" for their dog, you can look it up on the CHIC web site and confirm the results of all tests. You can also research the dog with its registered name even if you don't know its number.

Another sign of a good breeder is membership in the local breed club or the National Breed club. This suggests the person is interested in the future of the breed and in making sure that others are educated about it. It's worth finding the breed club in your area. It will be stuffed with people eager to tell you about their breed, both the good and the bad, and suggest people who might have pups available or a litter being planned. It's so easy to get sucked into a good web site, only to find out later that the breeder is a well-known puppy mill.

It's a little more subtle, but good breeders should be able to tell you why they have bred the dam and sire, and what they were hoping to achieve with the breeding. This will tell you that they are not just breeding indiscriminately, but that they saw an opportunity to improve the breed with the litter.

Among Dane breeders, people usually breed only one or two colors. Anyone with all the colors of the rainbow is someone who should be checked especially carefully. Beware of a Dane with a high price tag being sold as an "exotic" color, like a fawnikin (white dog with brown markings) or a blue fawn. While these are unusual and sometimes gorgeous colors, they are not acceptable in the show ring. These mis-marked dogs can be the product of perfectly acceptable color breedings, but they aren't worth more money just because of their color. This is true in Danes and other breeds that have more then one color variety. Of course, they can be great pets and are eligible for non-conformation AKC events, like rally, obedience, or agility.

Finally, try looking for someone who is active in some sport with their dogs. If they're not showing in conformation, perhaps they show their dogs in agility, rally, or obedience classes, or they track with them or take them to field trials. A good breeder is someone who believes not just in the dogs they have, but in the future. They want to get their dogs out in front of the public because they're so proud of them and their abilities.

If you are new to the show world and want a quality dog to show, try to build a relationship with people in your breed by going to the shows and meeting them ringside, or finding the local breed club and attending meetings. Your chances of getting a truly good dog will go up if people know you and can see your interest and commitment to the breed.

There's a new web site devoted to listing breeders of show dogs, run by Rita Suddharth. Drawing on her years of experience in the show world, she researches breeders before adding them to the site. Breeders must have bred dogs for show as evidenced by their web sites, catalogs and on-line results. You can find this site at: www.onlythebestpuppies.com.

Finally, you shouldn't be in a hurry to acquire a dog. Breeders don't breed on demand, they do so only when they think they can put together a sire and a dam that will produce sound, healthy puppies. Often they wait until their own life circumstances will allow them to spend time home with a litter of new puppies, who are a LOT of work. Bitches come into heat only twice a year, so no matter how eager someone might be to have a litter, they'll have to wait until the girl's ready. You should, too.

Please don't buy a holiday puppy: plenty of families are trapped with an unsuitable dog they get for the kids for Christmas. If you must celebrate a holiday or birthday with a pup, why not get a gift certificate for the kids that says they'll get that pup once you find the right one? Then they can participate in the fun of researching breeds, visiting kennels, and visiting on-line sites. This will help them to really understand what the pup will require and look forward to enjoying their new dog for its entire lifetime.

About the Author

Alxe Noden is a writer, photographer, and filmmaker, as well as the chief dog feeder and janitor at home. She has written two previous books, one on working for the federal government (while at the Center for Social Policy Studies) and the other on contemplative landscape design. She travels the country giving workshops and lectures with her husband on photography, landscape design, and meditation. She has owned dogs most of her life, though Kunga is the first dog she has ever shown. She lives in Boulder, Colorado, with her husband and her dogs. Alxe blogs weekly about her showing experiences and other dog-related issues at www.dellaspro-bono.com.

Dogwise.com is your complete source for dog books on the web! 2,000+ titles, fast shipping, and excellent customer service.